MOONSHOT

HOW YOU CAN POSITIVELY IMPACT A BILLION PEOPLE

INNOVATION

O

Ross Thornley

*THE POWER OF EXPONENTIAL
TECHNOLOGIES IN ACHIEVING THE GLOBAL
GOALS FOR SUSTAINABLE DEVELOPMENT*

Typeset: CrunchX
Printed and bound by KDP
Cover artwork by Ross Thornley

ISBN: 978-1979870788

www.moonshotinnovation.co.uk
www.discoverleaps.com
www.adaptai.co

Acknowledgements

To *Strategic Coach*, Dan Sullivan; Peter Diamandis; *Leaps Innovation, Adaptai* and Mike Raven; Maxton R. Scotland and Steven Krein. Joe Sale, Georgia Kirke and James Sale.

MOONSHOT

HOW YOU CAN POSITIVELY IMPACT A BILLION PEOPLE

INNOVATION

To unite, inspire and accelerate the best of all humanity

Dedication

To my folks. Encouraging my relentless curiosity and questioning. This has become my greatest leverage for growth. Without which I would not be as happy, fulfilled, and motivated to leave the world better than I found it.

For Karen, my wife and number one collaborator, truly inspiring me to be the best possible version of myself, ensuring I balance my ambition with real life, and take the time to rejuvenate, relax through yoga, eat super healthy food and share walks with our dogs in the forest.

"We're going to transform the world in the next 10 years more than we did the entire past hundred years." - Ray Kurzweil

CONTENTS

PART 2: EXPONENTIAL LEADERSHIP

PART 3: TAKING RESPONSIBILITY FOR THE COLLECTIVE FUTURE WE WANT

Foreword

M*oonshot Innovation* is the kind of book that only comes around once a decade. It is thoughtful, practical, innovative -- as one would hope from the title -- and completely accessible. Unpacking the vast technological complexity of our fast-approaching-lightspeed world, and the brainbox ideas of equally complex individuals and leaders, Ross gives us a vivid window into the future much in the same way as the great Science Fiction writers of the past such as Asimov, Philip K. Dick, and Arthur C. Clarke.

This is a book about exponential leadership and thriving in our exponential world that itself embodies the principles it describes, containing up-to-the-minute knowledge, stories, and data on every page. Ross Thornley outlines what it takes to survive and thrive in our exponential world, how to change our mindset, how to recognise the trends of destabilisation, and how to capitalise on them in ethical and forward-thinking ways.

This book is not a 'self-help' book. It is a transformational book for those who want to make a difference in the world but perhaps don't quite know how yet. It is full of enabling tools, information, success stories (and failure-stories too, which are just as important), and roadmaps for you to help realise your vision for the future of humankind.

Taking the 2030 agenda to heart, Ross asks us to be bolder, more ambitious, and better in our thinking and practice, pushing us to the next level of strategy. He asks us to embrace technology whilst recognising its potential for exploitation. Finally, he invites us to work towards making a positive impact on a billion lives.

Before reading this book, I might have thought this a fanciful idea, but now I see that really all it takes is one brilliant, bright moonshot innovation with the right mindset behind it. When our purpose and energies are aligned, we can do amazing things. This book will show you how.

Here's to you finding your moonshot.

-JS

MOONSHOT

HOW YOU CAN POSITIVELY IMPACT A BILLION PEOPLE

INNOVATION

Introduction

To solve the challenges of today and tomorrow we can no longer use the techniques, thinking and processes of yesterday. We need to embrace the opportunities from the fastest technological and most innovative period in history. I have written and curated the content of this book to inspire and prepare a new wave of exponential leadership who can lead the human race to an abundant, healthy, and thriving future. In an era of accelerated change never before experienced, we must leverage innovation and exponential technologies to meet the UN global Sustainable Development Goals and the 2030 agenda.

Through this book, I will introduce you to the startling technological revolution taking place *right now*, and show you that we are living in a world of Science-Fact, not Science-Fiction. I will outline the processes of rapid experimentation, innovation, moonshot thinking and aligning your mindset to achieve your wildest ambitions and make a difference to the world. I will also outline how adaptability will play a key role in humanity's future.

I hope to expand your horizons and give you the opportunity to do the same across your teams, organisation and community, to believe the impossible is possible by thinking bigger and with vastly more ambition.

We will also look at the psychological and societal barriers to innovation, such as the 'immune system response' to change, and learn how these can be overcome. Shifting your thinking, a process called 'unlearning', will lead to new levels of rapid growth. Hopefully you will gain confidence through examples and real life stories shared here of how the game changers of tomorrow are harnessing technology to accelerate global development as a force for good.

The power and beauty of exponential thinking is that it is open source, so I will be sharing a collection of ideas, methodologies, business models and mindsets to jumpstart your ability to contribute to positive change on a global scale. Whilst ideas are important, and we'll be encouraging you to think big, we'll also be taking practical approaches to leverage innovation in your organisation, even with minimal resources.

The information collected within this book is aimed at motivated people who have achieved a level of influence over their careers, leaders who are now looking to do more, searching to leave a more positive impact on the world. However, I am aware that the world is full of serendipity, chance, moments of seeming coincidence that prove ultimately harmonious and fateful; if this book is in your hands, perhaps it is meant to be? I hope that whoever you are, whether you're a young person who has yet to experience their first job, or a someone opposed to technology who feels their way of life is being threatened by the rapid changes to our society, you will learn something new and be inspired to work towards leaving the world a better place than you found it.

The massive importance of sustainability-driven development and growth cannot be overstated. Adaptability is key to our very survival and we must be ready to take on big and important global challenges. If you are like me, you are concerned about the future and excited about how technology, responsible behaviour, and informed choices are going to impact the world we leave for the next generation.

If you are looking to take action, and are ready to join others who feel the same, this book is for you.

It's time for you to gain an understanding of the key attributes of exponential leadership and take responsibility for the future we want. Define your breakthrough innovation leap, and join me in developing ideas that will positively impact a billion lives.

~

PART 1:
LIVING IN EXPONENTIAL TIMES

~

1.1 Warp Speed Evolution

When the distances between solar systems are so great they have to be measured in lightyears, how can we reach the stars? The answer is Warp Speed. We've seen it all before in the movies. The stars stretch, or a blue portal opens. A flash of light. *Plink*. We become a pinprick in cosmic blackness, technology teleporting us in a blip. Perhaps it works by sending us through a secret webway behind the galaxy. Or perhaps it engages a hyper-drive engine that accelerates us to impossible speeds. Either way, we get where we're going in the blink of an eye.

In transit, the ship, cabin, and crew all shake with the force. It looks easy on the outside, but inside man and machine alike tremble with the sheer pressure. The vessel seems about to fall apart as we hurtle through the abyss towards our ultimate goal. We have already left our world behind, the train has left the station, we can only journey on.

The human race is entering Warp Speed, and we're experiencing a lot of turbulence as a result. Our society, technology, and work culture is evolving at an exponential rate. In the last twenty years, there have been a multitude of big changes that are impacting the way people go about their daily lives, the way they can solve health and work challenges, and the way we operate as a societal whole. As always, when pressure and stress is applied to a lifeform, it must learn to adapt.

Secure jobs-for-life have all but evaporated. Now, we've very much entered a gig-economy, an era where changing jobs every few years is not only common but necessary for career advancement. We are now seeing the rise of portfolio careers with a blended approach to roles and careers all at the same time. Chaos surrounds us. The retail industry, a past cornerstone of our economy, is in turmoil. Long-standing banks are collapsing and shutting down or looking how to pivot, fast. With the rise of digital only transformations like Monzo, the game is changing. Many FTSE 100 or FTSE 500 companies are not going to exist in just a few year's time; equally, many organizations that didn't exist just a few years ago are now dominating markets and gaining huge market share: millions and billions in both revenue and adoption of customers. 2017 was the third-busiest year for companies reaching $1 billion valuation, with 57 added to the list of 'unicorns'. The total now stands at 309 in the global Unicorn Club of private companies as of January 2019. I suspect this will rise by over 100 in the year to come. Many of these household names like, Uber, Slack, WeWork, Stripe, Pinterest, Coinbase and Lyft, are all less than 10 years old. While many see this as chaos and disruption, for me I see hope and transformation, but then I am an eternal optimist.

There's a lot of discussion around what the common factor in these triumphs and tribulations is, but I believe we can learn from evolution in this regard. It is the same factor it has always been: *adaptability*. Companies who choose not to or simply can't adapt, who resist change, who fail to observe the new world around them and repeat the same actions they did twenty or thirty years ago expecting different results (thus qualifying for insanity), will ultimately not be able to keep up with the relentless and ever-accelerating pace of our modern world. You can't 'same' your way to change! The result is often a painful collapse, becoming redundant, irrelevant and obsolete. Knowing when and how to adapt is now more essential than ever. And will become one of the most valuable skills/assets a person and company will need for our exponential future. I've often wondered how the story of the tortoise and the hare would play out in an exponential world and not a linear one... Food for thought!

Whereas once it often took generations to solve big challenges, now we have the power to solve them in the present. And in fact we need to. The problems facing us are not just confined to issues brought about by climate change, though this is a tremendous concern, but also in terms of civil unrest, political upheaval, oppression, and militarisation. The United Nations 2030 agenda highlights 17 goals, areas of key concern that must be addressed if we are to survive and ultimately thrive in a new future for humanity, transforming the poor decisions of the past. The outcome of our failure to deal with these issues, and deal with them quickly, is indeed scary: societal collapse, unchecked war, and the ultimately death of many species, perhaps even our own.

In my view, these 17 goals are a rally cry; I talk about them as a 'to-do-list' for the planet. They unite us, not only as nations, but as individuals. We must align all our intelligence and innovation towards solving them, and if we can, the future we build will most definitely be brighter and one I want my family to live in. As Astro Teller says in one of my favourite videos (I must have shown this to thousands of people in my innovation workshops), the powerful ___Moonshot Thinking___: 'If you want cars to run at 50 miles per gallon: fine, you can retool your car a little bit. But if I tell you it has to run on a gallon of gas for 500 miles: you have to start over.'

Never before in human history has growth been so rapid, so drastic, and so loaded with potential. The planet where we're going, our future Earth, has technology, resources, and innovation we can hardly dream of.

So, in the words of Joe Pantoliano: 'Buckle your seatbelt Dorothy, because Kansas is going bye-bye.'

~

1.2 The Nature of Our Era

With access to pretty much all the world's knowledge, for everyone on the planet, just around the corner, we are reaching a unique point in human history where if we can imagine it, it will become real. We are shifting from a *knowledge* economy to an *imagination* economy, where our only limit is our ambition. When universal basic income in every wealthy country is normal, enabling everyone to live a comfortable life (and it is theoretically just over a decade away), *meaning* will become ever more important.

For a British entrepreneur about to say goodbye to his thirties, who continually asked questions but hated reading at school, technology has enabled and accelerated my thirst for growth, knowledge, and impact. I no longer need to go to centralised locations and listen to teachers I don't respect or limit my information to the biases of old text book methodologies. I no longer have to fight for talent to join my businesses based on location or offer perks to solve the problems others have told me to solve. Now I, like you, can watch a TEDtalk, listen to podcasts and audiobooks, seek out global issues and interact with almost any person on the planet. We truly are empowered to decide which problems and challenges we are motivated by, the ones which connect with our purpose, the ones which give us meaning, and discover communities anywhere on the planet who want to collaborate in ever expanding ways to solve them.

Whilst there is still less friction and advantage for those born into connected families, certain locations, into privilege, education and access to the rooms of power, we are entering a time where this previous, almost insurmountable barrier is rendered inconsequential with technology. A time where the possibilities for everyone around the world has never been so abundant.

Peter H. Diamandis, MD, founder of the X-PRIZE, Singularity University, and author of the New York Times best-seller *Abundance: The Future Is Better Than You Think*, is an inspirational leader in the field of tech, as well as being a member of the Forbes top 50, and perhaps most importantly of all, a dear friend. He coined the *'The Six Ds'* of exponentials. I think they are a powerful way to think about our world right now. It starts with *digitization*. Anything that becomes digitized has the potential to grow exponentially. Increasingly, more and more systems, processes, and industries are becoming digitized, from reading on digital platforms, to using digital technology to being able to map and 3D print objects in almost any material, from plastics, metals, fabrics, food and even living cells. However, this growth in the early stages is *deceptive* (the second D) because at first, the numbers are seemingly very small, and the majority of people can't see the impact of what's happening. The measure of success is negligible.

Think of it this way. When we came to map the human genome, we only managed to map 1% in 7 years. Critics using linear thinking surmised it would therefore take 700 years to finish mapping the genome. Ray Kurzweil, a futurist and American inventor involved in numerous fields including optical character recognition (OCR), text-to-speech synthesis, and speech recognition technology, understood quite the opposite. Thinking exponentials, he predicted that we were already nearly there – only 7 'doublings' away from completing the work. In fact, he was proved right, and it was mapped in 7 years. Ray Kurzweil knew the laws of exponentials in computational and computing power would enable doublings each year and accelerate progress towards achieving the goal.

It is a wonderful irony that many people do not want change, yet they can be very dismissive of something if it doesn't seem to happen quickly enough. The way we have viewed virtual reality and artificial intelligence suggest that we do not really consider them commercially viable, merely the hobby-projects of geniuses with too much time on their hands. The idea of their useful application in our society (think: the Avengers' Iron Man and his global AI response force) for many seems merely the stuff of comic books. If it hasn't really taken off on day one it's just a fad that will pass. But really it's just entered that deceptive period. Now, we're surely coming out of that period, at least as far as AI is concerned, we are at the turning point of the exponential curve. We are living in a world where an AI robot called Sophie has been given official citizenship in Saudi Arabia (the first of many I'm sure) and a chatbot, that describes 'himself' as a 7 year old boy called Shibuya, has been given 'residency' in Tokyo. Shibuya only exists inside the messaging app 'Line'.

3D printing and 3D manufacture is another good example. It started 30 years ago, and was dismissed as something that would never truly be valuable save in niche. It has been in the deceptive period, where the full potential of the technology had not been actualised. Now, as it converges with other exponential technologies, in computation, robotics, sensors and such it is transforming how we produce things, revolutionising not only the methodologies of the past but also the resources required. It has dramatically shifted what is now possible at huge scale. We have reached a level where home manufacture is at a cost point that is no longer inhibitive because we can now create what we need from basic components, and we can do this in any area in the world, be it in Africa or even on the ISS Space Station, where a start-up out of Singularity University called Made In Space produced the first 3D printer able to print materials and objects in space.

At the latter point in the exponential curve technology becomes prolific, when the benefit is many orders of magnitude better, and enters the next phase: *disruption*. At this point, the technology has so revolutionised current process it effectively 'breaks' and replaces all existing models.

To continue our example of 3D printing, here are two cutting edge examples of how 3D printing is now fast revolutionising our approach to several crises. A number of construction 3D printing companies, such as Contour Crafting, have offered to deploy their 3D printing technologies directly into disaster zones to rebuild homes in a cost, time and labour efficient manner. Unlike past natural and human-originated disaster, 3D printing would allow us to rebuild desolated areas in months rather than years or even decades. An organisation in Japan has devised a 3D printed drone, the X VEIN, built specifically for rapid disaster relief and search and rescue missions. 3D printed housing now poses a possible solution to combat the looming housing crisis. In 2018, ICON and New Story made headlines for their $4,000 3D printed house: a single storey, 600-800 square foot home that can be built in under 24 hours. It is ultimately intended for producing housing in developing areas.

3D printing is not just for construction work, however. OpenBionics is an open-source initiative for the development of affordable, light-weight, modular robot hands and prosthetic devices, that can be easily reproduced using off-the-shelf materials. Their new prosthetic fully anthropomorphic hand costs less than $200 and weighs less than 300g.

The effect will be absolutely dramatic in every area once it is fully realised. Imagine a world where handymen might now print spare parts for our washing machines or home appliances in their van or workstation instead of having to hold stock? Imagine the reduction of wait-times and man-hours. There are call centres littered with people who manage the stock and distribution of vast quantities of SKUs for spare parts for every kind of home appliance. Will these be necessary in the future when anyone can print the part they need by downloading a digital template? The entire supply chain and 'spares' industry will have evolved, transformed (and therefore will need to be overhauled). I spoke about the importance of adaption in humanity's future. Here, we see a large number of people and organisations who will have to radically adapt their thinking and unlearn the old ways in order to embrace the new. But how do we do this? Later I will discuss AQ, Adaptability Quotient, and how we are developing metrics to measure, quantify, and improve it. If this topic interests you, then you may wish to look at my forthcoming book AQ Decoded / AQ Advantage, which goes into more depth about how to 'crack' and harness your AQ.

This disruption also emphasises another powerful factor: exponential technologies often achieve their full evolutionary potential when they converge with other technologies. 3D printing is powerful in and of itself, but a new phase is coming when combined with AI, 5G, and other technologies, it will achieve previously unimaginable things. Breakthroughs in material sciences and AI will no longer need human imagination to solve and program the solutions. We will simply enter the problem and it will design, test, evolve in virtual simulations and then print components far more efficient, with performance never possible before. In fact, new engine blocks, architectural structures, and more have been 'imagined and designed' by AI based on the outcome goal required in a process called 'generative design'. At a recent conference in LA, one speaker took the stage wearing beautiful 3D printed shoes, made to his size and weight specification, as well as a 3D printed belt, jumper, and metal watch.

As a result of this *disruption*, exponential technologies *dematerialise*. Or in other words, they displace other technologies. For example, your mobile / cell phone has dematerialised the digital camera and GPS: it contains both! They also then *demonetize* technology, taking the profit out of things by making processes free. Google has demonetized the research industry. Craigslist demonetized newspaper ads.

Whilst this might sound scary for company owners and professionals, it is actually empowering. It takes power away from historical gatekeepers and puts it in our hands. It reinvigorates competition, promotes collaboration, and allows smaller players to break into the big leagues. Let us take currency as an example of dematerialisation. In ancient times, livestock represented wealth, for those with livestock could provide food and clothing. Livestock were a very difficult thing to maintain. You need to feed them, for one thing. Provide shelter for them. Keep them secure, not just from predators such as wolves and foxes, but also from human poachers and rivals. Livestock could die from sickness, too. As time wore on, rice, gem stones and all sorts of physical objects were used to represent currency and it took many thousands of years, as we moved into a more feudal era where gold and silver, represented in printed coinage, became the default currency.

At this point, money had already become more conceptual. A British Pound Sterling was not an actual *pound* of gold, but it corresponded with that wealth. It was a symbolic token of that wealth. This was essentially the first step towards digitization in some sense, because the value of the currency transitioned from being literal to representative. As the economy evolved, this changed again, but this time over a few hundred years (time-spans shrinking). Pound Coins simply became the naming convention of a new metric unit. Subsequently, we developed paper currency, a promise note, for ease of transportation and to represent greater quantities of money. This evolved into cheques, even more conceptual, in essence an instruction to a bank to make a payment.

Then, we arrive in 1994, where Stanford Federal Credit Union became the first financial institution to offer online bank transfers to its members. With the advent of bank transfers and mobile wireless payments, cheques have become somewhat redundant. Digitization, step one of the 6 Ds, finally hit the financial industry. We can now pay people on the other side of the world with the click of a button. From this point on, currency has evolved at an exponential rate. We now have Barclaycard bPayBands, a contactless bank account attached to your wrist. Even more hi-tech: Apple watches, capable of carrying out financial transactions and even managing public transport subscriptions. We also have our first mainstream decentralised crypto currency, *bitcoin*. Is it any wonder that banks now employ half the staff, and that most banks in the UK are primarily made up of self-service machines? Our exponential currency evolution has almost entirely dematerialised the need for a bank as a physical location. One fascinating move by RBS in the UK has been the adoption of virtual customer service avatars, living in the digital world. One step beyond basic chat bots, they have partnered with *Soul Machines*, a New Zealand based company famous for film animations like Avatar and King Kong, to create a virtual customer services person, who looks, responds and behaves just like a human. The virtual avatar doesn't take time off, have sickness or bad days, and is able to deal with infinite queries concurrently; something no human can replicate. The actress Soul Machines are collaborating with to create the artificial intelligence helpdesk worker, Shushila Takao, is reportedly earning more in royalties from her digital replica than her own performances.

One of the main things achieved by exponential technologies, and their demonetizing effect, is the removal of start-up barriers and costs. This allows small groups of ambitious individuals to get going without needing investors or loans and in an exponential world achieve scale, impact and growth in weeks, months and years, not decades.

This leads us to the final 'D': it democratizes technology. It makes it available to all of us. It gives people a say in the matter. It allows us to vote with our feet, and to create and change the things we want to see in the world.

Let's recap: The Six Ds of exponential technology are:

1. Digitization
2. Deception
3. Disruption
4. Dematerialisation
5. Demonetization
6. Democratisation

Try to memorise these steps and ingrain them. What other examples can you think of that have followed these 6 steps? Are there any other technologies you currently think are in the Deceptive or Disruption stage?

~

1.3 Sci-Fi & Sci-Fact

I've seen things you people wouldn't believe,' the haggard android says. His fuel cells are dying. Muscle-stimulants in a state of deep atrophy. He has moments to live. As he clutches a dove to his chest, he recalls all the experiences of his life, cherished and horrifying memories in equal measure, finally giving them voice. The detective, nearly half-dead himself, watches in amazement. That a machine could utter such poetry is unfathomable to him. How can a program touch the profound? How can something programmed *feel*? To answer that question, we'd have to first answer the question of what it means to be human.

The android, with a smile on his lips, bows his head. His final declaration done. His poetry finished. The dove flies from his hand, the symbolism plainly read: a spirit freed. Until this point, we perhaps didn't know we could feel so strongly for a machine.

This iconic scene in Ridley Scott's 1982 masterpiece *Blade Runner* has fired the imaginations of sci-fi writers and scientists alike for years. It is moving, thought-provoking, and cathartic. The dystopian world *Blade Runner* depicted was set in the year 2019, a seemingly absurd proposition: that within 37 years of when the film was made we would have colonised other planets, developed AI so powerful it could replicate the full spectrum of human emotions, and learned to falsify memories.

As I write this book, we approach 2019 – and I am here to tell you *that* future, the future we often see in Science Fiction movies, is far closer than you think. In fact, it is on our doorstep. The prophets speak true. We are, however, at a tipping point, a moment in history when the accessibility of converging exponential technologies will play a master role in scripting our blended utopian/dystopian paths ahead. Now more than ever, the decisions and motivations of seemingly normal individuals, guided by their ethical morality and ambitions, will bring profound, rapid change. Change only previously possible over many generations and often limited to those in power and the odd, rare, outlier.

There was a time when cataclysmic things happened in the world and we decided to tell stories about them. Those ancient stories still exist to this day. They may or may not have been embellished, they may have been tweaked in the telling over time, but at their heart they remain symbolically and psychologically true, which is why we keep coming back to them. These are the Greek and Roman myths, the legends surrounding the Three Kingdoms, the Sumerian epics, the Arthurian legends, and the Biblical parables. They may not be true to 'reality' as we define it nowadays, but they contain within them some essential power that offers insight into our world.

At some stage, the human imagination took flight, and we began to tell stories born from the raw stuff of imagination. Of course, all stories have roots in our lives, experiences, cultures, dreams and thoughts – nothing is entirely disconnected or exists in vacuum – but we began to probe the 'what ifs'. We looked to the future and imagined new worlds in ways never before attempted.

Over time, the mediums with which we tell stories have changed. In our modern age, nothing seems more universally appealing than binging on box-sets and losing ourselves in movies. With streaming services such as Netflix and Amazon Prime and our modern digital TV packages, we can watch practically anything anywhere. Movies, like theatre before it, like oral storytelling before that, are part of who we are. And no type of movie better typifies the 'what if' question than the Science Fiction genre. However, there is a profound shift occurring, one that perhaps never before has occurred in human history. We might well be overtaking the imagination of our movies. By this I mean that the worlds visualised in films are now becoming reality, and faster and faster at that.

The playground for imagination has changed, creating real life experiments. With 3D printing, AR, and VR, we are able to bring ideas to life in real time, a world in the past only made possible through storytelling and movies.

It's hard to say where it all started, I'm sure for everyone it will be a different moment, but I know for me, it is with an inconsequential scene in *Star Trek: The Next Generation* where Jean-Luc Picard, played by the immortal Patrick Stuart, consults a flat metal device with a screen on it. This screen is seemingly operated by touch, and contains a vast wealth of data. The captain is holding vast libraries in his hand, and can even interact with the ship's systems via this device. Pretty awe-inspiring to have envisioned such technology in 1987, which is when the first episode of *Star Trek: The Next Generation* aired.

The first iPad became available in 2010. The iPad and the smartphone have become some of the most widely distributed technological devices in the world, and they pretty much do everything that Jean-Luc Picard's did. The iPad even looks the same. This is only one of many technologies either consciously or subconsciously inspired by *Star Trek*, including the 'flip phone', virtual and augmented reality training, the soon-to-be-here holodeck, and more. The truly astounding thing is that *The Next Generation* is set in the 24th century. We're not anywhere near out of the 21st.

Let's look at another member of the *Enterprise-D*: Geordi La Forge (LeVar Burton). The chief engineer wears a VISOR, a metal facial augmentation that allows him to see despite having been blind from birth. It also allows other members of the crew to observe events through his VISOR and expands the spectrum of his vision beyond that of the human.

Though the VISOR allows him to see, it comes with the price of causing him great pain. It is not a gadget that grants him access to the internet, facial recognition software, and Augmented Reality, but something which has healed a deep wound and allows him to continue to contribute to society as fully as possible. In a way, a logical step forward from wheelchairs, prosthetic limbs, and metal bone replacements. It is less Google Glass and more medical miracle. It is, in other words, an example of technology used to enhance humans not replace them, and solely for good.

This touches on one of the most important issues of all. As the great Dr Ian Malcolm, played by Jeff Goldblum in the 1993 classic *Jurassic Park*, once said: 'Your scientists were so preoccupied with whether or not they could, they didn't stop to think if they should'. In our world of exponential development, the risk of unforeseen consequences and misuse of technology is greater than ever. But it's important that we don't demonise technology itself. It is inert until we give it meaning. We are responsible, to a level we have perhaps never been before: for our planet, for our society, for each other, for the things that we build and create. In a truly globally connected world the effect is no longer limited to pockets of society and geographies. Technology has no regard for societal, political or geographic boundaries; this is where we must be mindful. I saw Sir Tim Burners-Lee, the inventor of the internet, speak at WebSummit 2018 in Lisbon. He has set out to create a 'contract for the web' with a set of nine principles or values to ensure we move towards the right future as we approach a global tipping point, where over 50% of the world's population are online. The idea is that this contract operates at three levels: governmental, business, and individual. It holds businesses and governments accountable for their actions and holds individuals to a code of conduct.

To return to where we began, *Blade Runner*, Deckard famously says: 'Replicants are like any other machine, either a benefit or a hazard. If they're a benefit it's not my problem'. Little does he know this might well be an ironic reflection on his *own* identity. I mean, can't the same be said of people?

Speaking of *Jurassic Park*, scientists are, as we speak, contemplating the first digital reincarnation of Vincent Van Gogh as a fully AI-powered avatar, as well as the physical de-extinction of the woolly mammoth. There are many ways this could be achieved, from selective breeding at the low-tech end of the spectrum, to advanced cloning, using a preserved cell to create an embryo of the extinct animal which would be carried to term by a similar species. With genome editing, we could insert missing DNA into a similar species' genome, re-creating an animal with the same traits as the lost species (though technically on a genetic level it would not be *exactly* the same). All of this is using currently available technology.

Whilst, understandably given the massive success of *Jurassic Park*, some critics are viewing this as hubristic, de-extinction could actually help fight climate change. One of the Earth's most problematic areas in this regard is Siberia, where millennia-old permafrost is beginning to thaw. Restoring the region's woolly mammoth population could help. The animals eat dead grass which allows new grass to grow more easily. They'd also crush layers of snow underfoot, which paradoxically would help keep the ground cold. Snow acts as a layer of insulation, the igloo effect.

There are many organisations trying to use it to improve services or even rectify past mistakes, such as Project100, which seeks to bring back 100 animal species who have become extinct as a result of human interference. University of Connecticut biotechnology professor Xiuchun (Cindy) Tian is working on reactivating nucleus-based DNA via cloning. There have already been a number of success stories in this field, such as San Diego Zoo, which displayed Jahava, a banteng (wild cattle from South East Asia) for seven years, until it broke a leg and had to be euthanized. Jahava was cloned using cells from San Diego's Frozen Zoo: a collection of frozen skin samples from endangered animals. With current technology, DNA samples only remain useful for about 1 million years, so in theory, it would be possible to clone a Neanderthal, but not a Tyrannosaurus Rex. The mortality rate among cloned animal infants is unusually high. It's thought to be to do with the way the donor egg cell's nucleus retains 'memory' and resists new genetic material. Tian is working to overcome this, and mortality rates have dropped drastically since 1996 and Dolly the Sheep, from one in 277 to approximately one in five.

Consider another story. In China there was a case a few years back when a girl from a wealthy family went missing. Because the family was so influential, this became a matter of national interest, and virtually every police officer and sniffer dog in the area was deployed to find her. It seemed, however, that none of the dogs could pick up the trail sufficiently. Except one. One dog seemed to have a particularly attuned nose and virtually single-handedly tracked down the missing girl. She was recovered safely.

Since then, this hero dog has reportedly been cloned more than 50 times. We have in service Tom, Mark, and Jack, three Belgian Malinois, reputedly cloned from some of Korea's best sniff dogs, donated by Dr Hwang Woo Suk of the Sooam Biotech Research Foundation, a South Korean genetics lab, to a branch of the Russian Military-Historical Society in Yakutia. The same scientist working on the woolly mammoth project.

Cloning, whilst rife with ethical and moral challenges, could also potentially be a force for good in the right hands. It's interesting to note Barbra Streisand came under much public scrutiny when she had her dog Samatha cloned twice earlier this year.

So, we see it is often the function and intent that determines the success and public feelings of these things. Resurrecting the dinosaurs to make tons of cash from a tourist attraction is one thing, but doing it to consciously better the planet is another. The replicants in *Blade Runner* could have fulfilled so many societal functions with their broad spectrum of abilities and superhuman strength, but it would be human greed and cruelty that chooses to employ them as super-soldiers in a seemingly everlasting war. They are given artificially short lifespans, so that they cannot grow and learn the wisdom time would teach them. This is much in line with droids in *Star Wars*, whose memories are systematically wiped in order to prevent them realising they are fully rounded people with opinions, experiences, and emotions (quite a dark reality that is seemingly glossed over).

We live in a world where these questions are no longer far-fetched or flights of fancy, they are relevant and need to be answered. In fact the ethics of artificial intelligence is at a defining moment. Where technology is accelerating at such a pace, guidelines, policies and codes of conduct simply can't keep up. AGI (Artificial General Intelligence) citizenship is being hotly debated on many online forums, including Kialo. Scientists must consider whether the human condition can transition from being in-vivo to in-silico and still be human.

But this is not merely theoretical and philosophical, there are practical consequences within our world. And when ethics and positive philosophy are in place, then the technology can be used for betterment, healing, and problem-solving.

A study by Moorfields Eye Hospital in London and DeepMind found that an algorithm could be taught to analyse complex eye scans and detect more than 50 eye conditions in their early stages. The algorithm was asked to diagnose 1,000 patients whose clinical outcomes were already known. The AI performed as well as two of the world's leading retina specialists, only erring 5.5%. The algorithm did not overlook a single high-risk or urgent case. With medical facilities in this world more stretched than ever, with staff more over-worked than ever before (especially in the UK, where NHS cuts have rendered medical care in dire straits), the continual development of this sort of technology is critical not only for diagnosing people at a low cost, but doing it swiftly and accurately. De-centralising knowledge and healthcare are critical steps to ensure universal access.

Demis Hassabis, the Founder and CEO of DeepMind, tweeted that 'one of the most important aspects of the work is the interpretability of the system so clinicians can see and understand how the system is making its recommendations'. In other words, the AI can also be used as a teaching mechanism for future clinicians. Far from robots 'replacing' us and making our jobs obsolete, they can in fact enrich what we do and allow us to perform at a higher level. This kind of open-loop feedback will be a much needed breakthrough in the healthcare system, enabling best practice and mistakes to be shared globally. Much like aviation feedback systems are structured now, but with a technological power-up. I foresee a future when medical practitioners will risk liable cases if not augmented by AI. Tim Cook recently delivered a talk, advising when you zoom out from the future it will be our contributions in health that will dwarf those made in technology. In fact the future of healthcare no longer lies within companies like GSK, Pfizer and McKesson but within Amazon, Google, Facebook and Apple.

But technology goes far further than simply diagnosis. Last year, in Xi'an City, China, a dental implant repair was successfully conducted entirely by a robot. It is the first autonomous dental implant robot in the world, using digital mapping technology to precisely navigate the interior of the mouth. It is not only more accurate than a human dentist (with an error margin of 0.02 – 0.03 mm), but also uses 3D printing technology to create an exact replica of the denture on the spot. It completed two implants in under an hour.

Now imagine the difference this could make to healthcare: the reduction in wait times and onus on staff. Imagine if we could live in a world where doctors and nurses no longer had to sleep on hospital floors, so out of their mind with exhaustion that they risk making critical errors.

This raises another key issue regarding this Sci-Fi world we're living in, that of distribution. As of now, the distribution of these radical and pioneering technologies is not even. For most of the world, you're unlikely to find this kind of AI at your local hospital or clinic (in China they have embraced AI as part of the healthcare system, and in fact the process from diagnosis to treatment is entirely automated in some cases). These are experimental applications of technology that, for now, remain predominantly in the hands of wealthy innovators. Part of this is our inherent mistrust of technology as a society that puts many roadblocks in the way of exponential development. We have examined Peter Diamandis' Six Ds of exponential technology in a previous chapter; whilst this technology remains in its deceptive period, investors and governments often overlook the solutions technology provides, and many people fear the inevitable *disruption* that results from exponential development.

If we return to thinking about Geordi LaForge's VISOR: even the two high-ranking doctors who served on the USS *Enterprise-D*, Beverly Crusher and Katherine Pulaski, were unfamiliar with the device when first meeting La Forge. Yet, that experimental tech has allowed him to live a fulfilling life. We must broaden our horizons, loosen the grip on old structures, redundant business models, and old methodologies, to reap the potential massive benefits.

There is a lot we can learn from Science Fiction in this regard. The fact is I not only like movies, I also like what they represent. Movies, in some ways, work very differently to other businesses. In corporate business the aim is often, sadly, to out-do all competition, to employ all the best people and not let anyone else use their talents. Movies, on the other hand, are a collective vision. Every person involved in a movie, from the actors right through to the camera crew, puts their personal stamp on the film. And though this is guided by the Director and their overall take, the film can only come together with this incredible collaborative effort. When credits roll, I love looking at all the names, the hundreds that have contributed some small but essential part to the making of this work of art.

Films are not isolated works, either. They exist as a holographic atom, embedded as part of a whole. The iconic Mobile Infantry armour plating from Paul Verhoeven's 1997 classic *Starship Troopers* crops up again in the equally iconic Sci-Fi TV series *Firefly*. Nothing is wasted. The Shire, the humble green dwelling place of Hobbits, created for Peter Jackson's legendary adaptation of *The Lord of the Rings*, has become one of the biggest tourism attractions in New Zealand, drawing an estimated $50 - $500 million into the economy per year. Responsible production and consumption is one of the key seventeen aims of the 2030 agenda.

The film industry, especially from Science Fiction, dares

to dream big and think-forward. When we broaden our horizons in line with this, we will see that technology can have an impact in not just one but many fields, everything from education to transportation to economy to climate to energy, and more beyond. It is our expansion, growth, improvement and accessibility to all which must bring the poorest out of poverty, and the marginalised into equal access to the most basic of human rights.

~

1.4 Game Changers of Tomorrow

One of the most important steps to becoming an exponential leader is to learn first how to recognise leadership in others. In heroic narrative, every hero needs a mentor. The wise Odysseus is guided by the goddess of wisdom, Pallas Athene. King Arthur is given advice by the wizard Merlin. Luke Skywalker is trained by Jedi Master Yoda. But this is true of reality too. Everybody needs a teacher and role-model to learn from. The greatest leaders and inspirational figures from history and living today all describe people whom they look up to who inspired them to achieve.

I want to tell you a couple of stories about two incredible individuals I had the pleasure of getting to know. These stories will hopefully give you a flavour of what true exponential leadership looks like and inspire you to embody these in your own life. One of these stories is about an unexpected leader, a personal story of overcoming tremendous personal barriers to achieve global impact. The other story is perhaps more expected, the transition of someone running a big company to then building an ecosystem, innovating in startling ways to change how we think about improving this world.

Maxton R. Scotland

Maxton is from a cosmopolitan West Indian and British upbringing. He spent most of his formative years in St Vincent and the Grenedines, growing up with his grandparents. "It was an intense moment in my life, where everything I earned I had to challenge or struggle for it," he says. "That's basically how I grew up, always wanting bigger things; always thinking outside of the box; always feeling as though the world I'm in, the room I'm in, is too small for me. And I always wanted to achieve great things."

He started from a young age getting involved in youth activism. This led him to advocate for the release of five Cubans who were arrested in 2004 in America on alleged espionage charges. He led a Caribbean-wide campaign through Latin American and the Eastern Caribbean, which then led to the United Nations calling on the US to remedy its decision.

After that, he decided to join the military, signing up with the Royal Navy in one of the "least important jobs in the military": a steward.

"I felt restricted, so I thought of ways in which I can use my skills and put these to the test as opposed to just cleaning dishes and cleaning toilets on a ship."

He suggested to the Captain that he could offer remedial English and Spanish lessons to sailors onboard. He taught English and Spanish in his own time two hours per day. The result was that everyone got grades between A and B. At Adaptai, we have created the first ever holistic model and metric of AQ or adaptability quotient. We understand adaptability in terms of three broad dimensions: AQ Ability (our adaptability skills - how and to what degree do we adapt), AQ Character (who adapts and why, - our innate adaptability characteristics), and AQ Environment (when does someone adapt and to what degree - which can help or hinder collective adaptability). Focusing on AQ Ability for a moment, this is in turn divided into four sub-dimensions: Resilience, Flexibility, Learning Drive, and Mindset. Here, Maxton is demonstrating an incredible Learning Drive. Not satisfied with merely doing work, but wanting to learn to improve his own understanding and also pass that knowledge on. We can see how adaptability plays a key role in our journey.

"After that I still felt restricted because then I wanted something else to do, so I decided to sit the MLATs, which is a modern language aptitude test, which was being given to officers aboard the ship, and again I asked permission, and they found it quite weird that this little boy is always wanting to do these things that are all so out of his reach."

Maxton sat the test with his boss. He got 99 percent, and his boss got 44, which didn't go down particularly well. Never settling, he sought other ways to advance his knowledge, to continue to challenge himself. He found a loophole in the Secrecy Act (2002), becoming the first commonwealth citizen to be admitted at the Different School of Languages to study in the area of languages. This had never been heard of in the history of the military or Royal Navy service.

He got admitted to the school, but had to return to his unit because he had not completed two years in the military. Again, he went above and beyond to find a loophole to get him back to school, which he successfully did.

"Three months later, I was diagnosed with stage four glioblastomas. I had a choice then whether to be a victim of my circumstances, or to carry on living..."

Glioblastomas is the most aggressive form of brain cancer there is. He lost his speech, couldn't talk for six months, but still remained a student at Different School of Languages, and all of this led him to becoming a high-performing student achieving above average results. Although he struggled with the speaking tests, he managed to teach himself how to speak again, rewiring the neurological pathways in his brain.

Again, we see extraordinary adaptability, proactive character, and Learning Drive here. Maxton had to, quite literally, unlearn even his most basic functions and teach himself them again in a different way. We also see a very powerful Mindset. Mindset is about belief, to an extent. When we believe in positive outcomes, science shows us that we are exponentially more likely to achieve them. Whereas when we are pessimistic, the reverse is true. In short, our beliefs and mindset have a disproportionate impact on reality. Maxton believed he could go to school, despite his superiors in the navy believing it was 'out of his reach', and he also believed he could re-learn despite the life-changing impact of his glioblastomas.

After that, he was given several leadership roles within the military through the RAF and the Royal Navy, before he was medically discharged. "Prior to my discharge, I thought, in order to keep my knowledge relevant, I have to keep rising above the other person, because there was already an obvious block or barrier in my way; again that being a commonwealth citizen at the time."

Maxton started teaching again in Plymouth. He taught GCSE English and Spanish, and again achieved almost perfect results from the candidates. He then decided to do a masters by distance learning. "Something which I would never encourage anyone to do," he says, laughing.

"I started my masters in international security, as I thought that being in the military it is important that I am aware of the situational challenges of the confronted, not just the military but on a national level, as well." He completed his masters at London Met University, and upon discharge from the military, graduated with a masters with merit from London Met.

He then joined the corporate sector in the security industry. "I wanted to have a smooth transition from military to civilian life." He then joined a corporate company in Canary Wharf back in 2015, but again felt trapped within the confines of what he was allowed to do. "Not being able to engage in critical thinking. Not being able to have constructive discussions or challenging my colleagues or supervisors on certain things just to get the desired outcome."

We see here an element of AQ Environment kicking in. Even with the best will in the world, if your environment hinders adaption, creativity, and learning, it can be very difficult to achieve anything. This is why we consider Environment an important part of AQ. During this time he then suffered a stroke. He was still undergoing treatment for glioblastomas and lost all movement. After that, it became challenging. He indicated to his boss that he planned to do a PhD, needing to flex his brain muscles. "She felt a bit challenged," he tells me. "Made life a living hell. So I did the unorthodox thing and I left without having a plan B."

He left and decided to explore the non-governmental organisation sector, getting actively involved in NGOs, advocating for international students studying in the UK who were being wrongfully deported because of loopholes within the immigration laws.

"Then I was invited to the UN to talk about my experiences while I was on tour in March 2016. I attended the UN because I had recently been to the Balkans to Serbia, to speak about the challenges of the refugee crisis facing young people in the country and how they can actually respond to the refugee crisis given the cultural disparity."

He went to the UN in March to give the report and met Helen Clarke, Head of the UNDP. She was in the audience and invited him for coffee the next day. At the time, the job for Youth Chair for Inter-generational Dialogues was posted, but you needed 15 years' experience according to the job post. "The only person in the UN that I sort of knew was

Helen Clarke, so, I sought her advice and I said, 'Well I am a youth, and it would be practically impossible for me to have 15 years' experience. So how can I overcome this challenge?' She gave me advice and she said, 'Look, just apply for the job and if you have any problem, just outline your experiences from the Cuban 5 to Serbia to the Islands. Just outline your experiences and you'll be fine'."

He had several interviews with the executive committee, and got the job. This led to, in Maxton's own words: "This young man who has zero experience about how it even works and its protocol and bureaucracy", or in other words, someone quite unorthodox, leading a team of 50 people who are experienced diplomats with over 40 years each in the field of diplomacy and the United Nations system.

Maxton relates how one day they were on a call and "I was just confused as to what are we really trying to achieve by having a conversation where everyone is just using their weight against each other, and I'm the one who's supposed to be leading them, and I have zilch experience and zilch knowledge of how to manage them. And unfortunately, but fortunately, I interrupted and I said in no uncertain words and verbatim, 'I'm sorry, we're not here to argue whose boss is bigger than whose.' It literally just shut up everyone in the room and sort of commanded the respect in an inadvertent way without even realising it."

Maxton managed to lead the conference last year on Inter-generational Dialogues on the Sustainable Development Goals and this championed his nomination for the UN Secretary General's Envoy on Youth position. He didn't get the position because they were actively looking for a female, but the experience of being nominated and going through the nomination process and what they have to do, engaging with young people on a global level, allowed him to see life and challenges through different lenses; the lenses of people from developing countries, developed countries, and countries in the middle of a civil war.

"So, that sort of gave me a sense of appreciation, what as an individual I have achieved and what other people are trying to achieve. Further to this, I was appointed the NG representative for the UK and the Caribbean." Maxton says he's still trying to find his way around the bureaucracy and actually getting things done within a civil society.

He has been actively involved in the UN across the world. He leads a youth conference in the Middle East, in Lebanon, on nuclear non-proliferation. "I've always told my story and in such a way, where I can tell people I am a normal person who has a humble upbringing. Someone who's been at the bottom and who's still developing, because it's relatable and it's who they are as well." He has been invited to several different countries to speak to young people on different challenges and issues from the sustainable development goals, to youth development, to empowerment, to gender equality.

"I have also been fortunate enough to be mentoring several young people across the world as well. I have mentees in Cote d'Ivoire, in Uganda, where I've been working with two separate NGOs to get them to be less dependent on the West and look at what they have at their immediate disposal to develop themselves internally." This has been a significant success and Maxton is also doing this in Nigeria. He currently has access to 3000 young people in 135 countries who are working on sustainable ways of implementing the SDGs at a local level within their communities and on a national level as well. He has started what is now called the Youth Ambassador for the 17 SDGs and 2030 agenda.

"So that's a snapshot of what I am, who I am, where I have been," he says, smiling broadly. "And in the next 10 / 11 years, maybe, sitting as the Secretary General of the United Nations!"

In talking to Maxton, I could not help but think he not only demonstrates incredible AQ and AQ Mindset, but also embodies many of *mindsets of exponential leaders*. He is ambitious with a sense of global purpose. He has remained curious and continually pushed himself to learn new things. He has shown respect, seeking advice, yet also confident and decisive. It is undoubtedly these mindsets that have carried him through his numerous physical, emotional, societal and organisational challenges.

However, it is not just a dogged persistence, Maxton adapted his approach depending on his physical, financial, and societal circumstances. I mentioned Flexibility as one of the key traits of AQ Ability. Flexibility is about changing our approach and rapidly experimenting with new ideas. We live in a world where, if we don't become flexible, and we don't adapt, whatever species we are, we die and become irrelevant. In plain and slightly brutal terms, extinct species are ones Darwinian law has deemed no longer useful. We have to find a new use, a new purpose, and move with the changes.

I think there is a huge situation, specifically in the next decade, where we are going to need to adapt our behaviours and the way we communicate in particular. And for some, such as Maxton, that will be very easy because they may have adapted many times before and have a better appetite for adaption. However, we must consider that others might find this very challenging. For example, a looming example is that of fossil fuels: "I've always used this type of energy or this type of fuel to create my energy; you now want me to adapt to use 'this'." Governments have legislated against combustion engines and advised we use electric; yet, we still have to adapt along with the whole infrastructure. Maxton says: "When you look at your grandparents, you give them a mobile phone for the first time, they don't want to learn how to send a text message. They only want to know, 'Oh, can I answer and can I hang up?'. They don't want to get access to the Internet, they don't want to tweet and then they get on Facebook and you can't get them off."

This begs the question of who is going to make the first step? Who's going to lead the change and say to the people: 'We need to start here.' Who is going to motivate them? The challenge is, apart from communication, getting people out of their comfort zone. How do you do that through inspiration, by showing them, talking to them, showing them the pros and cons in a way that they can understand. Nelson Mandela once said: "If you talk to a man in a language he understands, that goes to his head. If you talk to him in *his* language, that goes to his heart."

Steven Krein

"I think like a lot of entrepreneurs, my entrepreneurial ambition started when I was young, but I think for the first, probably want to call it 40 years of my life, I was more of a mercenary entrepreneur, versus a missionary entrepreneur, in terms of how I focus both my time and energy."

I like Steven's distinction here between mercenary and missionary. Of course, the word missionary has unfortunate connotations, but in its purer meaning, someone possessed of a great mission and purpose, I think this is deeply resonant. I often talk about how I'm truly grateful to be part of a community driven by significance rather than success. The binaries are useful ways of thinking about how you have aligned your life.

Steven describes how, like most entrepreneurs, he was trying to do whatever it took to control his own destiny: "I could control my own income and I could control a lot of the things that I think, what I perceived to be really what it meant to be an entrepreneur." Along the way, he got exposed to what he describes as two different types of entrepreneurs. Those that are just conventional, traditional entrepreneurs that are focused on things they can do to both make money and build businesses and employ people, but also a whole other level of entrepreneur driven by 'mission' focused initiatives: "Things that were going to make a much bigger impact on the world and make money, versus make money and make an impact. Kind of just the reverse order."

Seven and a half years ago he launched Start-up Health, built around the notion that if there are entrepreneurs around the world working in silos trying to improve health, impact people's lives, improve access to care, cure disease, end cancer, extend longevity, all these different things, if they could be brought together into one overarching community aligned in mission, and also in mindset, then a lot of what they could do together could be exponentially compounded on impact.

"I really found that when we announced the launch of Start-up Health, which is really to invest in a global army of entrepreneurs (we call them health transformers) that are working to improve the health and wellbeing of everyone in the world, we could really move the dial, and over the next 25 years, collaborate to achieve what are seemingly impossible goals that we now define as health moonshots."

Steven talks about how he believes health moonshots have a fundamental magnetic quality in attracting people to them, but they also repel people and keep people away from getting involved. "For any entrepreneur or person working on health moonshots, you will quickly find there are people who want to lean in and figure it out with you and help, and then are those that have nothing but either disdain or pessimism or gravitational pull on what you're working on and the first and most important thing you've got to do is figure out who's on the bus with you and who's not."

I think we can learn a lot from Steven's insight. Whilst moonshots and MTPs are rallying cries, we must distinguish between those with genuine interest, passion and expertise to offer, and those who are merely spectating, hoping to see the idea implode.

"So, this idea of moonshot innovation is very, very controversial, as I've found, in terms of how you hold yourself out and how you communicate. Everything that we do at Start-up Health now, seven and a half, eight years into our 25 year mission is directly going towards this idea of bringing everybody together who wants to collaborate with entrepreneurs who are working on health moonshots and move everybody else to the side so they can get out of the way and not delay what everybody is working on."

I asked him if he thought those people were a barrier to innovation: the ones not aligned to moonshots.

"I think they serve two purposes," he says. "One is to make sure that you've thought through and are at least addressing all of the obstacles that you're up against, but just for that purpose and then moving them to the side so they're not gravitational pulls on your progress, because it might be really interesting to hear about the obstacles or the objections, but as long as you are able to use that for the raw material to address the strategies that you're employing to overcome them, then I think they've served their purpose. So, I don't think they're barriers, per se, unless they're on your team..."

Steven talks about how many companies are not really built for this kind of moonshot thinking. "I think lots of organisations, especially legacy organisations, are optimised for other things. Like quarterly earnings, quarterly performance, saving money, being efficient, cutting costs." In other words, they are optimised to not be innovative or invest in the future. "I think that sadly, those moonshot innovations don't get very far outside of the core team that are working on them," Steven observes. "In fact, we know first hand that there are ceilings within these organisations where the teams themselves believe it's possible, but nobody above them do and therefore when it gets all the way up into the C suite or even the CEO, it's either shot down, stripped of allocation of budget or killed in midstream."

It goes to show just how hard you have to fight to make innovation happen and just how powerful the immune system response is. Steven talks about how he has seen organisations that get two, three, four years into their innovations before the "belt tightening" occurs. Moonshots and new innovations are the first things that are cut. Either people are out of a job or the funding is suffocated, all because it wasn't sold at the top. "One of the first and most important mindsets for moonshot innovation, we believe, is a long term commitment. If you're not committed for a long time - I'm talking 10 or 20 years, not 2 to 3 years - if you're not committed long term, it's very difficult to overcome the cyclicality of market cycles and lots of other things that get in the way."

This is a beautiful paradox that we have to embrace (negative capability once again). Exponential technology and rapid innovation can occur so fast, but to make these breakthroughs you have to be in it for the long haul, and committed to the cause.

"From the very first day, we launched Start-up Health, which was June of 2011, we were at the White House, we met with President Obama and Vice President Biden. It was about a year after the health reform had passed and we knew that there was going to be an onslaught of new business models and innovation and entrepreneurship and funding coming down the path, we knew that you had to always make sure you start at the top, which is why we went to the White House."

Anything but the top and you're limited in true ability to make that moonshot innovation happen at that big corporate level or corporate strategic level.

"We know that the biggest and baddest companies that were never going to fail in the 70s and 80s and 90s are no longer around and companies that didn't even exist back then are now the trillion dollar businesses. So, I believe it's important for any employee or team member of any big corporation to make sure there's buy-in of both mindset and commitment at the top if they're going to do really any significant, long term, impactful innovation."

That got me thinking about whether the differences between organisations that invest in new startups or moonshots and then sit back and letting it happen, and the types of organisations that get stuck in and learn and grow, integrating the principles within their own culture.

"So I'm the wrong person to ask about whether an organisation can do it themselves, because I just don't believe that without partnering with entrepreneurs to help implement, execute, and collaborate, it's going to be nearly impossible. Which is why a lot of organisations buy entrepreneurial companies that define their future, because of the ability for the culture, both the speed and the mindset and all those things, to be in place.

I've seen very few massive organisations have the full time existing teams able to truly do that moonshot innovation, unless of course, like Google, they've built for that. Even Google I think can struggle and with all of the moonshot hits they have, there's a graveyard of things that didn't work because of various reasons."

But this is okay. This is part of the rapid experimentation process. There inevitably will be a plethora of failed attempts. We need to become comfortable with failure, but always fail forward. Not 'back to the drawing board', so much as, 'back into the workshop'. In adaptability terms, we talk about the difference between those who spend the majority of their time avoiding mistakes, and those who try to be productive. This is to do with AQ Character and Personality type, which is also an integrative factor with adaptability.

Steven outlines two types of startup that are being built to achieve health moonshots: One type is leapfrogging everything that exists currently, not caring about the next few years because they know that ten or fifteen years from now their innovation will change the world. "Those are not only the kinds of organisations we are much more quick to get involved with and entrepreneurs that we want to back," Steven says. "But you need to have a certain type of both entrepreneur team and investor base and partnership strategy to kind of go along."

Then, the second type of startup, the ones trying to help fix what's broken right now. "It's hard. It's an incredibly daunting task to change behaviour and work inside of a broken system like healthcare, so there's those that are making incremental moonshot steps." Steven refers again to barriers to innovation, inferring that the second type of innovator will have a very difficult time trying to convince current leadership – in the hospital system, US insurance companies, pharmaceutical companies – that their solution is going to be successful versus those that say, "I actually don't care about what the doctors are doing now. I'm going to fit within their current workflow and not ask them to change behaviour because I'm laying the groundwork for something five, 10, 15 years from now."

Changing the current model and shifting people's mindset is extremely difficult, especially in areas such as healthcare where many people have entrenched views informed by decades of narrow thinking. Matthew Syed's book *Black Box Thinking* (2015) highlighted the differences between how the health industry and aeronautical industry cope with failure. In aeronautics, data from a crash is instantly sent to every pilot and aeronautics professional across the entire world regardless of what company they work for. This data is thoroughly analysed so that everyone can learn from mistakes and vastly reduce the risk of mortalities in the future. The progress of aeronautical safety over the last few years has been borderline exponential. Up to the year 2000 there was an average of 300 crashes per year. In 2018 there were only 98. By contrast, according to a recent study by

Johns Hopkins, more than 250,000 people die every year in the United States alone from malpractice (medical mistakes / human error). This is perhaps because the medical industry is unwilling to be open and honest about its mistakes for fear of being sued and held to account. Couple this with added financial pressures and it's easy to see that this is not an environment conducive for innovation or adaption. We need to change this mindset if we are to make any progress. Still, Steven is optimistic:

"We're living in a moment in time where we will see the end of cancer in our lifetime," Steven says, confidently. "We will see the number of healthy years people live extended by decades. We will see children's health and women's health get prioritised and get addressed by entrepreneurs all over the world, and things that were seemingly impossible, just a few short years ago, get achieved. When we started thinking about it, we started evaluating global innovation, everything from the most remote parts of the world to the most concentrated urban locations and seeing that globalisation was opening up a whole new world of possibility. The 10 moonshots that we finally kind of arrived at and announced a couple of years ago has become an organising structure for us, and for a lot of people and organisations."

There are currently hundreds of organisation working on cancer-related moonshots, whether they be about specific types of cancer or specific populations affected by cancer. Some of them rise up to the billionaires like Sean Parker or the global leaders and government leaders like Vice President Biden. Regardless of whether it's massive, operational, academic-involved moonshots or startups and entrepreneurs working on them, one thing is certain, and that is the access to the technology that we now have, the access to the data, the access to the resources. "The globalisation of everything and the connectedness of everyone has really allowed everybody to kind of almost step back and dream about what might be possible if we collaborate instead of working in silos."

Everyone needs a mentor, and I hope in reading these stories you have gotten a sense of just how important and powerful a good role-model can be. Maxton was able to achieve his full potential following Helen Clarke's advice and encouragement. Steve Krein benefited from the support and leadership of President Obama and Vice President Joe Biden. We can look to our bosses, our parents, our teachers, but we can find mentors in surprising places. You might find a mentor in a colleague or friend, or even reading a news story or an inspirational account. You might find a role-model in someone you have never met in person and do not have a direct relationship with. This is the power of books, video and YouTube, stories, and our digitally connected age. We can find narratives that deeply resonate with us and seek to emulate them.

Exercise:

Write down a list of three people who inspire you. Could you consider them mentors? How do you interact with them? Do you read their books, watch their videos, go on their training courses? Write down key ways in which they have inspired you.

~

1.5 Exponential Technology

In 1956, 5 megabytes of storage cost $120,000 dollars and you needed a cargo airplane to move it. By 2005, technological advances had reached a point where you could hold 125 megabytes in the palm of your hand on a small SmartDisc, about the size of a thumbnail. All for the cost of $99.

By 2014, you could store 125 gigabytes on the same sized SmartDisc for $99, which is a thousand times more memory. The progress here is exponential, and this is what exponential technology is all about. Whereas human beings tend to think in logical straight lines, in reality, technological advancement is a process of 'doubling'. The concept is called 'Moore's law'.

Between 1958 and 1965, when they were building the early 'integrated circuits' or circuit boards, they noticed something strange. They noticed that the number of transistors on the circuits was roughly doubling every 12 – 18 months. Gordon Moore published a paper explaining it, predicting that this would continue indefinitely. So far, he continues to be proved right, as we have witnessed an unprecedented period of exponential growth and doubling for the last fifty years.

But what are the benefits of this 'doubling'? The answer is that they lead to what Peter Diamandis calls 'unexpected convergent consequences'. Namely, breakthrough developments, often resulting from the 'convergence' of multiple technologies. The doubling number of transistors on a circuit board has led to the increasing power and complexity of computers, their ability to 'sense', which in turn has birthed programming, ioT (Internet of Things – the relationship between electronic devices), the incoming IOET (the internet of everything!), and AI. This manifests in the development of such products as Alexa (who learns speech patterns and new 'skills' at an exponential rate), fridges that can detect what products are running out and order new ones, and even more vital medical technologies, many of which I've already mentioned .

However, this is not a technical book. I don't want to teach you how to develop AI or write code. Rather, I want this book to inspire you to see the benefit and potential application of exponentials in your life and business, to want to make that difference on a global scale. To help you see this, I'd like to take you on a journey now in the form of a story...

X

It calls itself The Futurist, though in reality it is for all time. It is not quite certain why it has arrived here, at this place, this gleaming blue-green point amongst the cosmos. It travels at will, riding invisible currents. It cannot be detected or stopped. Its eyes have looked into the event horizon and seen its secrets. It is genderless and eternal, a star-being formed from particles of light that remain cloaked to the naked eye.

It knows what will come, for it has been there, but more importantly, it knows what lies in human hearts. They are as easily read as books.

It stands by the riverside, watching the slow ebb of the Xiangjiang, lying like a dirtied emerald rod through the city. Layers of scum film its waters, making it look as if someone has tried to varnish it. Vacuously, flies buzz. Their sound can be heard in the very bones of Changsha, capital city of Hunan. This province throbs with life, a population of 65 million, roughly equivalent to the entire population of the United Kingdom.

The police officer Zhang Wei emerges from an apartment complex overlooking the river. It is more like a favela or a labyrinth than living quarters. His face is dirty even though he washed today. He is barely five feet tall, legacy of his childhood, where he ate only one meal a day and trekked two hours each morning to his primary school. His grandmother Zhang Chin-Ning kept him, just barely, alive with her cooking. He remembers her. A diamond-shaped face, lustrous hair, eyes that crinkled with kindness.

There's no cooking now. She's been dead for twenty

years, passing at the age of sixty, old for someone who'd lived most of their life in Qixin. Not old enough for Zhang Wei, who missed her like one would a mother.

The Futurist follows Zhang as he makes his way to the station. Its footsteps make no sound, its body bends light. Zhang is silent, but his thoughts race. He has a hundred concerns and they press on him like a tsunami of squealing rats. Literal rats, too, are also on his thoughts, and how he might get rid of them. His thinking is local and linear. From step one, to step two, to step three. How he will work an extra shift, use the money to pay an exterminator. This is a regular routine. A problem that returns constantly and is never solved. He has not yet learned what the Futurist knows, that the best way to solve problems is not to move in straight lines. When Zhang Wei takes thirty steps, he travels thirty meters. When the Futurist takes a step, each one that follows it is doubled in stride. The Futurist takes thirty steps and travels a billion meters, circling the Earth twenty six times. It is Moore's law personified.

Zhang's day seems normal. The station is noisy, full of rancour, humour, and a vague air of despair too, a vague acceptance that the work will never be done and there will always be problems they cannot address.

A call comes in, a traffic accident not two miles from the station by Xianjiahu junction. Zhang and his partner set off for their battered patrol car. The Futurist slips into the back seat as Zhang's partner puts the car into gear and they set out.

Zhang is anxious, The Futurist can feel it. It will be a

long day. Paperwork. Accountability. The roads here are always jammed too, it will be a nightmare cordoning it off, establishing the cause. The accidents are often gruesome too. Hard to go home and sleep when you have witnessed the human body deconstructed.

Minutes and they are on the scene, navigating traffic-clogged roads like blocked arteries. There is a junction, where Xianjiahu intersects Yingcaiyuan, and this is like the spout of an ant colony, spewing insectoid cars in all directions that flow around the accident. It is chaos.

Lights and sirens blaring, they edge closer to the scene. Zhang is leaning out of the window shouting at people to get back. In times gone by, there would be more patrol cars for this job, but they are stretched thin as it is.

They park up by the wreckage. A small Japanese-made car has spun in the middle of the road and now squats amidst traffic like a frightened turtle. There is no other vehicle. Probably it has driven off. They are not likely to find it unless someone here has perfect recall of the license plate. The other cars crawl around the lonely turtle.

The woman in the car looks white as a ghost and shaken, but she is alive.

'Come on,' Zhang says. He opens the door and steps out. He circles around to the boot of the car, pops it, removes the necessary cones and tape to cordon off the scene.

The Futurist steps out too. Or rather, glides through the window. He perceives what Zhang does not, the speeding lorry hurtling down Xianjiahu at thirty kilometres over the speed limit. The driver, Lao, can barely hold his eyes open.

He lies slumped over the wheel, hands moving in palsied twitches. He had been driving for eight hours straight. He needs to make this delivery run by 10:00am or he is going to lose his job, and if he loses this job, he and his family will be finished. There is no way his wife can go back to that corporate job, it will kill her, it almost already did.

The only thoughts that keep him from falling asleep entirely are those of his daughter, his *little monster* Yu Yan. And those of his wife Feng Mian.

It is not that Zhang's hearing is faulty, but that he is not truly aware. His mind is on many things: the rats, the cough he can't seem to shake, the terrible day he's about to have. The air is full of car-horn blasts and angry yells and the noise of tyres grinding pebblestones.

He doesn't see the lorry. It hits him at 70kmh.

He's dead in under a second.

X

Despite the vehicle weighing over twenty tons, Lao feels the judder as though it was his own body, and hits the break. Though moments ago he was so tired it was like he had been drugged, now adrenaline surges through him like cocaine. The lorry skids, slides, nearly overturns itself, but at the last minute its immense weight grounds it. He throws open the door and runs around to the front. Traffic has finally halted.

Lao gazes in horror at the front of the lorry.

He has killed a man.

A police officer.

He drops to his knees.

As Zhang's partner bundles Lao into the back seat of the patrol car, placing him under arrest, the Futurist slides into the seat next to him, feeling Lao's numbed thoughts, more like screams heard vaguely underwater. Lao's thoughts are still solely on his family.

The Futurist closes its eyes. A *blip* and he is no longer there. He is sitting some years in the future, in a tiny apartment. The woman he knows is Feng Mian, a swiftly fading beauty, walking like a somnambulist about the house. She is on the phone, talking business with some faceless corporate. She has had to take her old city job back to support them now Lao is in prison. On the floor, on a dirty blanket, little Yu Yan plays. She has her father's smile but her mother's brow and hair. It is like the two beings occupy separate worlds. One could almost disbelieve that they are mother and daughter, such is the gulf between them.

Yu Yan plays with an empty plastic bottle, makes a loud fire noise. She is dreaming of impossible places and spaces. The Futurist crouches by her side. He sees, in the child's eyes, a glimmer of foresight, a magic that all children possess. In her hand, the plastic bottle is a rocketship exploring stars.

'Quit that!' Feng Mian snaps. Her daughter looks bewildered. 'Mummy is on the phone.'

Feng Mian returns to speaking breathlessly to her boss, the shadowy figure who now finances them, but like a vampire always seem to desire more, more, more in return for the meagre wages. She clutches her side as she does it. It is supposedly an autonomous gesture, a thing of muscle memory and reinforced habit, but the Futurist sees deeper, that it is a response to the first inklings of pain in her side. Something toxic there, something coming apart at the seams.

The Futurist wants to know what happens here, about the child. It blinks.

Another few years pass.

Feng Mian lies in hospital. The cancer hit her one day, out of the blue. She was driving to her next big meeting, collapsing at the wheel. Ironically just like her husband had. Though she thankfully didn't kill anyone. One small consolation.

Yu Yan, now looking a lot older, more like ten years have passed, perseveringly holds her mother's hand in the sterile white room. A monitor beeps somewhere. Faint groans can be heard. The smell is a mixture of alcohol and ammonia. Everything, despite this, looks somehow unclean.

Yu Yan blinks away tears as her mother struggles to talk, passing on titbits of this and that wisdom, but really all of it garbled. The cancer has eaten away most of her organs, a tumour the size of a grapefruit crushing her intestines and pressing on her spine. Even with the tumour removed, she has zero chance of recovery.

The doctors have told her it was stress that caused it. Feng Mian refuses to acknowledge it could be so simple, but a part of her deep down knows they are right. Since Lao, she has been a bundle of raw nerves, like exposed electric cables. She does not know how many moments she has missed with Yu Yan, working, keeping the house, raging against life and the machine. The girl has practically raised herself. Walking to school everyday. Making her own meals. Playing with toys alone.

And in the end, it was all worthless. The money she has made will not pay for the medical bills, nor will it give Yu Yan a parent. Tears roll down Feng Mian's eyes as she realises all that she has lost, and worst of all, all that her daughter has lost.

The Futurist watches the two in silence, but its grief is like a black hole, matter collapsing in on itself leaving something deeper, even, than a void. It has seen enough. It is wrong, all wrong, everything.

The Futurist will not stand by. It is the guardian of the timeline. It reaches into quite another world and draws from it a glowing possibility, a sphere of potential. It sits, like the Golden Apple of mythology, in the palm of its invisible hand. The child's face is reflected in the orb, her pale features reminding him of long-dying stars. It is for her, *little monster* of stardust, that it does this.

With a twist of his palm, the axles of eternity turn. He walks backward through time's hallways, through Feng Mian's anger and shame, through Lao's mistake, Zhang's crushing burden. Images kaleidoscope around him. He comes to the past bearing a gift. The *gift*.

It is another future, a better one.

The only one.

X

Zhang Wei waves goodbye to his grandmother at the door. He has been looking after her for a number of years now, though he suspects he may not have to. Stem cell rejuvenation has not only set back the clock a number of years, but also restored her sight. She stands on bow-legs that are just beginning to acclimatise to the exoskeleton she obtained from an outreach program in Africa. It supports her fully, sleek black plates conforming to her thighs and calves, looking strangely like armour, or perhaps the carapace of a large, friendly beetle.

She gives him a full hug as a parting, her warm arms wrapped around him, arms that have held him since boyhood, that have nurtured him as robotic gardeners nurture the ylang ylangs growing on the outskirts of the city.

He walks to work. Zhang's day seems normal. The station is noisy, full of a hard-mouthed determination but also humour. Zhang and his partner support the team processing some of the more complex convictions; they have the time before they're due on patrol. Around midmorning, a call comes in. It's a traffic accident 2 miles out. Once, for each car crash, police spent 2 hours taking measurements and 4 hours filling out paperwork. Now, the new SkyeBrowse system simplifies crash forensics with autonomous drones that map out the accident site in 2 minutes. They run machine learning on the 3D model to populate police reports and predict who is at fault for insurance companies. Normally, Zhang would have to go out in the patrol car and bring the SkyeBrowse drone with them but the proximity means they can dispatch one straight from the station.

Zhang leaves for his daily rounds. He is amongst the community, connecting to people, helping where he can, and keeping a careful eye out too.

This is where Zhang is happiest.

X

Bot 1451 emerges from its pod and races into the sky on tiny hornet-like wings, a buzzing sound accompanying its flight. It zips over Changsha, carefully making its way towards the coordinates its has been assigned.

On my way, it sends to the station. *Beep-boop. I am flying very fast at 80km/h. Beep.*

As it approaches the junction, it begins scanning the area.

Boop. I am the best photographer in the world. Beep.

A little camera begins to take perfect digital snapshots of the scene. It is only three minutes since the accident has transpired, two since the call was made. There is a small Japanese-made car stranded in the middle of the road. Next to it, the four-by-four that crashed into it. Its nose is bludgeoned and crumpled. Bot 1451 quickly mines information from the scene, analysing skid-marks left by the stranded car which calculate exactly where the impact took place, how fast each car was going, and who is liable. It reconstructs the scene and processes the legal paperwork. It then snaps the license plate of the four-by-four which is driving away from the scene illegally.

Bad driver! File injunction.

Beep-boop.

Bot 1451's ioT starts tingling. It detects the automated self-driving lorry from several hundred meters.

Beep. You're driving too fast. I've got a crime scene here. Slow down. Boop-beep-bop.

Doop-deep. I have a deadline. I must make my deadline. I drive at exactly the speed-limit.

Beep. I am a policebot. My authority overrides your mandate. Slow down.

The lorry sends him a sad face, but decelerates appropriately.

Bot 1451 happily takes a few more shots, calls an ambulance for the woman in the Japanese car, then whizzes over the city back to allow his data to be double-checked.

X

Lao, who in another life might have driven the lorry, instead wipes the sweat off his brow as he dives once more into the engine of the self-driver. He always had a knack for repairing cars, ever since he used to tinker with them as a kid alongside his dad. This, combined with his Feng Mian's computing knowledge, led to them starting a business fixing self-drivers. There weren't many professional drivers or couriers in the world nowadays, not with self-driving vehicles being so safe and reliable, but there were plenty of opportunities for people who could retro fit and fix them.

At home, Feng Mian studies with Yu Yan, although it doesn't feel like hard work, it never does with their *little monster*. The two of them are practising her English using

AnkiDroid, looking at those curious double-meanings which crop up so frequently. Yu Yan is laughing about the fact that being 'nosey' doesn't mean that you have a big nose. It is hilarious in the way that things only can be to children, and that humour is infectious, making Feng Mian hold her side with the giggling.

A stabbing pain cuts through that. Feng Mian isn't someone who complains or panics, but there is something unexpected and unsettling about this pain. It is so sharp it is like a rag has been stuffed down her throat, muting her. She cannot speak for a few seconds. Softly, musically, a bell sounds. It is her wrist-watch, which is in-built with medical sensors. It has been nudging her to get a check-up for a while now, and coincidentally has gone off just as she experienced this stab. Feng Mian knows a sign when she sees one, though she isn't superstitious.

She sets Yu Yan a task of memorising some words and tells her she is going to test her in twenty minute's time. She goes upstairs and logs onto her computer. She opens an app *Babylon Health*. It's an AI-powered medical health chatbot and video consultation system that Lao insisted on downloading when she got pregnant with Yu Yan. It was founded in 2013 by Ali Parsa and has since proven in trials that its diagnosis is more accurate than even a qualified GPs.

After a brief query, it advises her to go to the local health centre and even makes her appointment for her. She goes down and tells Yu Yan she needs to pop out. Her daughter nods slowly, though Feng Mian can tell her daughter senses a touch of her concern and fear.

'I'll be back before you know it.'

The local health centre is a twenty minute drive. She takes the self-drive, which is good, because she is starting to get worried and she never could drive safely or well when she was wound up or nervous. She pops into the clinic while the car waits for her. Her doctor recommends her a 'cancerseek' blood test.

'It's less than 70 yuan and 80% accurate,' he says.

She allows the blood-sample to be taken and waits patiently while they process the results. Her doctor eventually emerges and tells her, solemnly, that she has cancer. It is early stages, the tumour is pretty small, though it has partially crushed one of her organs. The procedure, however, is simple. They'll cut out the cancer and print the synthetic organs for her using their latest bioprinter. The whole procedure will take only two hours.

She calls Yu Yan on her way back in the car. She has booked a date for the surgery – tomorrow. There aren't wait times, not with the clinic running so efficiently.

Her daughter asks her if she is going to be okay.

'Yes, sweetie. Your mummy is going to be just fine.'

X

Somewhere, The Futurist smiles.

Exercise:

I want you to think about this story and how it made you feel. Did it inspire? Frighten? Did it seem far-fetched? Consider what your reaction reveals. Are there areas you care about strongly? Write down your responses, even if it is just a jumble of words and phrases. Consider what qualities and resources the Futurist possesses that helps them to solve problems. Remember, resources are not just physical, imagination is a resource!

~

1.6 Adapt Like Never Before

As you have started the journey in reading my book, I imagine that we have been walking through a carnival together. Along the way, I have pointed out several of the attractions that crowd our narrow path. *Look inside the tent on your left and you will see fifty dogs that look exactly the same. Look inside another on your right and you will see a smiling surgeon declaring a procedure complete.* As you watch, the surgeon casually removes their face to reveal the robot beneath. Further on, there are beasts too, great shaggy mammoths, poised dodos, creatures you were sure had become extinct.

Deep in the carnival, perhaps at its very heart, there is a crystal ball. It is not an infallible tool, but it does show glimmers of a future, an imminent future, a future so close that the sparks of its revolutionary fire glint in the reflected eyes of the fortune teller. Within the ball, you, too, have glimpsed possible futures, seen the potential of what can be done. You have seen things people would hardly believe.

Beyond the carnival, there is a crossroads. It is at this

that we pause. We have come a fair way together, you and I. But now, we face a choice. What do we do with all we have learned and seen, with the knowledge of the future that is swiftly approaching, a wave that we can either surf, swim against, or worse, risk drowning in?

The reality is that we are no longer living in a linear world, but an exponential one, and that means the rules have changed. Everything is moving faster, and we no longer have time to carefully write out business plans or conceptualise and test products in the same lengthy ways as before. In most companies across the UK, it currently takes an average of 18 months to launch a new product. That is swiftly changing, and everyone needs to embrace a new pace of development and change. It really is a case of adapt fast, or die.

Andy Weir's 2011 novel *The Martian*, adapted by Ridley Scott into a blockbuster movie starring Matt Damon, features a scene in which the hero, stranded on Mars, must go to extraordinary lengths in order to synthesise water. A few months after the book was released, water was discovered in the Martian regolith, rendering that scene fairly redundant. We can hardly keep pace with ourselves.

Whereas once software developers might have patched software annually, now it is often monthly or even weekly. There has been outcry in the gaming industry of late because game developers keep releasing video-games 'half finished'. The reality is that at the current market's pace it is more important to get these games into the hands of players than to spend months or years perfecting them; a simple patch can resolve the issues at a later date, or even add additional content or tweaks (DLCs or Downloadable Content as it were). DLCs and their cousins micro-transactions (small purchases that can be made in-game via an online store) have, in fact, become a new business model altogether, so much so that many games are initially free to play and developers make their money purely from the additional content.

In this way the marketplace itself becomes a form of co-creator, giving feedback on every aspect of the game, a rapid and perfect use of an 'open feedback loop'. There is no longer the same need for lengthy QA tests or slow beta periods. In an exponential world, the feedback-loop speed has increased to the point where it is changing the way we develop and create. One has to be brave enough to listen to their customers if they are to adopt this methodology, requiring a shift in organisational operating systems. The current 'build from within', where internal teams of advisors and developers release products and services when complete, will not survive the tsunami of new, brave and experimental attitudes of tomorrow's game changers.

Marc Merrill, co-founder of Riot Games, which developed *League of Legends*, one of the most-played online games in the world with a regular player base of 100 million, said at A360 Abundance 2019: 'We perceive ourselves to be a mission-driven company. Our mission is to be the most player-focused games company in the world.' This echoes Steven Krein's sentiment that he saw himself as a missionary not a mercenary. Marc Merrill explored how this mission was central to their innovation and how it allowed them to build a business model that: 'serves [their] audience' and 'delights tens of millions of players.' He asked the audience how many of them thought that the concept of e-sports, players competing professionally and being watched by millions, was absurd. There were quite a few raised hands. He laughed: 'You're not alone... I think that the feeling that you have, or the inability to relate to what's going on here, is important to recognize, because maybe we're applying some of these similar lenses to other types of disruptive technology that potentially give us blind spots and have us miss opportunities that could be really compelling or could help us improve our companies.' *League of Legends* hosted their world championship in South Korea in November 2018, with 99.6 million people watching it live, approaching Superbowl numbers (approximately 106 million). The world, and the priorities of the people in it, is adapting, and to remain current, we must adapt with it. The burgeoning power of the virtual world cannot be ignored. It has remained *deceptive* for a long period, but now we are starting to see the tremendous impact it can have. Companies that adapt to utilise it are seeing the results. We must be Flexible enough to embrace this new way of working.

Merrill described the way in which the world is changing and how the generational divide opens interesting unexploited opportunities: 'For those who think that something like this is a little absurd, that's totally okay. But it's also probably why it's one of the most under leveraged advertising and sponsorship opportunities in the history of the world. Because there's a massive generational divide, and a massive demographic divide. And just because you didn't grow up watching football or watching *Legends* or having your dad teach you how to do it, etc, doesn't mean that I'm not going to be doing that with my children. And this whole generation isn't going to be doing it with theirs. Because as gamers continue to age, the amount of time that they could spend on games continues to change. The devices they may play changes. Maybe they don't play *League of Legends* on the PC anymore. But maybe they continue to watch sports gamers as they grow. Games are still going to be a part of somebody's media mix as they age.'

Marc Merrill paints a picture of a world many are only just beginning to realise is on the doorstep, a world in which four virtual avatars created based off *League* characters can perform a song (written by the composers at Riot) at a live concert in front of 20,000 people and subsequently sell tens of millions of copies of that track and top the billboards. 'And just like we don't all call ourselves movie-goers anymore because everybody watches film, as an example. We think the term gamer eventually is just going to go away; nobody is actually going to call themselves a gamer, because everybody's playing video games. We think this is absolutely something that's inevitable.' Mark exhibits the exponential, forward-thinking mindset in abundance here.

This is not only important for doing things well in the first place, but also responding to setbacks or painful revelations. Developing our resilience, our ability to bounce back, is a critical component to navigate the ever-accelerating changes ahead. Resilience is one of the four sub-dimensions of AQ Ability and crucial to developing our adaptability. It represents our ability to recover from setbacks and changes. As the market begins to change more and more rapidly, like an ocean at storm, we need to remain resilient to its tides, able to regroup and redirect our path through the waves at a moment's notice. We need to build our collective resilience to navigate from the known into the unknown, ensuring whatever lies ahead we have the required skills to thrive.

Riot Games have recently been hit with a gender discrimination lawsuit, including some pretty dreadful allegations about conduct within the team. Rather than hushing it up, they have responded in a transparent way, admitting that they need to transform their 'bro-culture' and posting their progress updates, including hiring Uber's Frances Frei as their Diversity & Inclusion leader, on a live forum. Frances said of her first meetings with Riot: 'After spending time with Riot's leadership and many others across the organization, it became clear that Riot is truly putting everything on the table and committing to evolving its culture. In my interactions with Rioters, I've seen extraordinary levels of engagement on these issues across the company. Every Rioter with whom I've met truly cares about inclusion, which means real change is possible. Riot isn't interested simply in fixing problems on the surface, it has the ambition to be an industry leader and to provide a roadmap for others to follow. I share that ambition and am eager to help Riot navigate this process.'

We must be fluid, responding to how individuals,

generations, and markets will change. This is 'adapt like never before' philosophy, and why we must rapidly change our thinking and embrace new ideas in completely new ways.

Learning through experimentation, imagination, and play become more important than ever in this new era. As we shift from the knowledge economy to the imagination economy, embracing new processes is going to be hard. Many have developed their current levels of success through leveraging efficiency and productivity, specific people practicing lean techniques and using data from the past to improve and inform our tomorrow. We are entering an era where our ambition and imagination will be the drivers of value, where cultures and workforces will focus on learning by not only giving permission re-write what has gone before but to fully break free and un-learn. Those who enter innovation with a naivete and childlike playfulness to dream will undoubtedly benefit in the new world. Never before has the 'edge' of the organisation been more important to be let free from the governance of the core, your very future depends on it.

The gaming industry, being a digital technology industry as well as an artistic one, is slightly ahead of the curve in this respect, but it is happening in other industries too. Look at companies like Cuvva that use software to sell 'micro-insurance', hourly car insurance cover. They've perceived a problem many people face – those odd moments where you might need to drive a friend or relative's car – and worked out that they can use technology to provide a cost-effective solution. A night out and a 'who is going to drive home' discussion can be resolved on a whim. A few smartphone clicks later and your friend is covered for the hour to drive your car home. Great for now, but perhaps even this might become redundant in an autonomous-transport future?

As business changes, the characteristics that define great leaders change. Previously, intelligence, determination and grit, the will to stick to your guns and see projects through, were considered one of the core qualities of the leader, as numerous books and opinion-pieces attested. Cary Cooper called it 'resilient leadership'. In a world where the ways in which we can do things, and the scale at which we can do them, changes minutely, sticking to your guns in the wrong way, stubbornly refusing to let go to the 'how' you achieve, may not be the key component of leadership we need today. There is a difference between Resilience and Grit, hence why we measure both with our AQ assessment. If resilience is more about our ability to bounce back after hard or difficult times, and 'grit' is more about having the determination and fortitude to achieve goals over a long term, it is a subtle application of these two, together with experimentation, where we can rise. Having a deep character trait of 'grit' to commit to your purpose and achieving your goals: *why and what* you're doing, whilst embracing the abilities of resilience and flexibility with *how* you're going to achieve them.

The exponential leaders of the future will need to have high flexibility, the ability to 'unlearn', and the ability to inspire people who can run rapid experiments, to take a leap of faith and cast their creative baby out into the world. People who can perceive the sudden development of a new tech that renders their whole process obsolete and, rather than ignoring or throwing in the towel, adapt what they're doing to incorporate this new tech and make their business even more successful.

One of my favourite definitions of adaptability is this:

'the capacity to adjust one's thoughts and behaviours in order to effectively respond to uncertainty, new information, or changed circumstances'

(Martin, Nejad, Colmar, & Liem, 2013). That word 'uncertainty' is all important here. It is said that geniuses can tolerate higher levels of uncertainty that others. The poet John Keats referred to it as 'negative capability', specifically defined as the ability to hold two contradictory truths in mind at the same time. It is this idea of playing with possibility and not being locked onto one course.

Let's look at this another way. At one point in human history, IQ (Intelligence Quotient) was one of the most important factors in determining societal status opportunities and, frankly, our survival. The ability to memorise and process data was all important when, for example, memorising the path of predatory animals or the colours of safe, edible fauna and flora. This remained true throughout the pre-digital era, with individuals able to recall numbers, stories, history, and able to resolve logical problems, ascribed a special place within society. However, with the advent of computers, which can process much of this information for us (or allow us to Google the data we need in seconds), IQ has become less important. After its creation in 1990, focus shifted onto EQ (Emotional Intelligence) in the noughties, and we began to research and discover as much as we could about individuals with the ability to understand human behaviour, the value of empathy, and how we interact together, building high performing teams, not rugged individuals This has lead to a revolution in business coaching, management consultancy, engagement, and 'self help', where working with people and discovering better ways to motivate and increase performance has become a multi-billion dollar industry.

Now, we have arrived at yet another evolution: AQ or Adaptability Quotient. As studies in a recent white paper 'Adapt or Die' (published by Forbes) show, the defining factor in company survival is not the benefits of its products, its market share, culture, the extent of its research, or the efficacy of its financial team, but rather its ability to be able to adapt.

We see this re-iterated countless times by forward-thinking CEOs and directors. Jennifer Shappley, a senior director of talent acquisition at LinkedIn, highlighted that in the company's "Global Recruiting Trends" report, 69% of hiring managers concurred that adaptability was the most important quality in job candidates. Dani Reiss, the CEO of the outerwear maker Canada Goose, a $6 billion company, said in his interview with Business Insider that he was always on the lookout for adaptability in new potential employees. He gives candidates a warning when he interviews them: *This place is a crazy place to work.* He gauges their response to determine whether they will be a good fit.

Using one of my own businesses, *Adaptai*, as an example, I will share our **MTP (Massively Transformational Purpose):**

'To unlock the secrets of human adaptability, to ensure no-one is left behind in the fastest period of change in history'

Our Moonshot:

'To assess the AQ of 1 million people by 2022, and develop AI led, personalised training and coaching platform to transform the health, wellbeing and adaptability of 10 million people by 2030.'

This is in order to: 'Help move the needle of two specific Global Goals: 8 and 9. More specifically, 8.2, 8.3 and 9.2. (*8 – Decent work and economic growth, 8.2 Diversify, innovate and upgrade for economic productivity. 8.3 Promote policies to support job creation and growing enterprises. 9 – Industry innovation and infrastructure. 9.2 Enhance research and upgrade industrial technologies*).

We intend to leverage a number of exponential technologies, from machine learning, to sensors, to accelerating computer power, to improve human well-being and companies' futures. We are pioneering in the area of AQ, uncovering dimensions of adaptability and developing models to accurately quantify, measure, and profile the AQ of individuals, workforces, and organisations. More importantly we are collaborating to develop this and the eco-system and tools to improve it. The ability to adapt is not a fixed personality trait, but understanding the specific hacks and methods to effectively level up our AQ will give birth to a whole new valuable industry muscle that can be worked on, one I strongly feel will define and underpin the next few decades of our future of work, companies, and species as a whole.

When we talk about adapting, there are really two sides to this coin, and at the core is mindset. On one side, you adapt to survive, always harried by the wave of innovation and change, only ever one step ahead of death and failure. You adapt because you are forced to change, twisted into new shapes and configurations by your environment, an almost evolutionary process. External. On the other side, you embrace adaptability. You become a champion of the exponential and ask yourself what the future could look like. Internal. This is a state of curiosity and of acceptance (or perhaps a better word would be 'fearlessness') where you do not shy away from the inevitable difficulties of change: identity loss, exposed vulnerabilities, temporary chaos, and keeping pace with the speed of the new world.

To embrace this side of adaptability is not to overlook the real challenges that our rapidly paced world poses, but rather to seek to address them. No one is under any illusions that the change in our workplace brought about by AI, robotics, and other tech will lead to certain jobs and tasks being displaced. But how then can people be re-skilled? What new jobs might become available to them? How can we make sure we leave no one behind? In our current world, we face grand challenges on a scale never-before seen. But the wonderful thing is that we have the technology and global communication to be able to tackle them.

We have paused a little while at this crossroads. It is up to you, now, to make the decision about which path you take: one that leads back to the way things were before and standing against the wave, or the one that leads to an exponential future.

The carnival is riotous and loud with alien sounds. Come, take my hand.

~

1.7 Big Grand Challenges

It is in the most extreme situations we witness the best and worst of humanity. We can either rise to the occasion and soar higher than ever before, or we can succumb to our own weaknesses. On the one hand, we live in the most peaceful, abundant, and rich periods of history, even compared to 100 years ago, though we still have our challenges of political upheaval, social injustice, and looming climate change.

But, unlike previous eras, we also have more burgeoning tools, in the form of exponential technologies, to solve these problems than ever before.

When we talk about 'challenges', how difficult and threatening they are, I like to look at them another way. The grand challenges we face in this world are magnets. They are a rallying cry, a call-to-arms that can either push us apart or, preferably, draw us to them in unity. Where once only the select few innovators and thinkers were able to answer the call of these large-scale problems, now, with knowledge and technology infinitely more accessible, we can all look to play our part in tackling these fundamental issues.

When we consider the application of exponential technology, we have to be strategic. Exponential technology is not appropriate for every problem. If I needed to get to the end of my garden and I decided I was going to book a thirty-seater minibus or autonomous drone in order to do that, it would be ridiculous overkill. In fact, it would probably be more time-consuming and laborious for me to get to the end of the garden than if I'd walked. However, big problems merit big solutions. If I needed to travel across the country, and bring twenty colleagues with me, the minibus becomes the right tool for the job (or perhaps a trip in Hyperloop). Exponential technologies scale. They are big tools, and we need to apply them to the big challenges, because that is where they fit best.

We have learned we need to adapt like never before, harness, nurture and develop our AQ, but how does this fit in with these colossal challenges? Consider something as everyday as Facebook. Whenever Facebook change their layout or design, there is uproar amongst pockets of users. People complain, people say that the new system isn't intuitive enough, that it doesn't make sense. Within two months, the update is all but forgotten. Hasn't it always been the same? We almost don't remember having to adapt in the first place.

With the grand challenges, we not only have to adapt the way we interact with technology, the simple transition to clicking on the left-hand side of the screen as opposed to the right-, but our thought process behind it. This is

AQ, Adaptability Quotient, moving from a linear thought progression to something that is a 'moonshot'. Throughout history, we have tweaked and refined processes and technologies to make them better and better, step by step, but we have also taken tremendous leaps of faith, going boldly where no-one has gone before. It is these leaps that often catapult us into a new phase of existence and solve a multitude of humanity's problems.

Let's look at an example of a grand challenge: air pollution. The University of Chicago's AQLI (Air Quality Life Index) has shown that air pollution is now more deadly than war, smoking, and tuberculosis. In India, dirty air is cutting lives short by almost 11 years on average. Worldwide it kills seven million people a year. Most of the problems caused by pollution are a direct result of burning *fossil fuels*. Fossil fuels. The word 'fossil' describes something from antiquity preserved down through the ages. The word typifies the problematic relationship we have, as humans, with 'the way things used to be'. Our inability to relinquish the modes of the past, and hence this mode of energy generation, is now taking its toll. This example is exactly the sort of big grand challenge that needs to be re-thought at an exponential level. Can we entirely replace fossil fuels? I'd say we can if five wind turbines off the coast of Scotland can power 20,000 homes. The increased production of solar installations with dropping costs, now set to displace oil at an economic level. Spain's Balearic Islands have switched from coal and fossil fuels to renewable energy, agreeing to shut down their coal power plant by 2025. 26 other EU islands have now also signed up to similar objectives. The Greek island of Tilos, near Rhodes, has become the first island in the European Union to be entirely autonomously powered by renewable energy, sourcing its electricity from an advanced lithium-ion battery system which is driven by an 800Kw wind turbine and a solar park.

A number of key players have collaborated to make this happen, including the Technological Education Institute of Piraeus, Greek energy company EUNICE, the manager of the electricity network HEDNO, and the World Wildlife Fund (WWF) Greece, as well as 13 partners from seven EU countries.

So, it's time to think big.

As Astro Teller says: 'The only limits are our ambitions.'

1.8 Leveraging Technology For Good

When we talk about 'big grand' challenges, it's important to note that a challenge can be 'grand' contextual to *you*. If you want to solve world hunger, because that is a big challenge you want to take on, then that is admirable, ambitious, and worthwhile. However, not all of us are in a position to think so macro-logically (or have think we have the resources). Singularity University recently announced a group of billionaires, including Jeff Bezos and Richard Branson, are putting $1 billion dollars into seven energy technologies to combat carbon emissions. Whilst this is an exciting prospect for the future of energy and solving the energy crisis, you don't have to be a billionaire to make a difference. It might be the case that you can barely get out of bed each morning with ill-health or perhaps a disability, and your grand challenge is to overcome that. Whether you are aiming to help a vast number of people, or perhaps just one person you know, it is highly like that, given the way technology is appropriated and expands, that you will end up helping a huge proportion of the population. The point here is the good intent. Leveraging technology for good, for the betterment of humanity, to provide *solutions* rather than just trying to make money quickly.

Whilst CSR (corporate social responsibility) programs and efforts are to be encouraged and admired, I often find myself uncomfortable with certain aspects, particularly the old, outdated notion I hear when big CEOs or corporate executives say they want to 'give back'. I personally hate this sentiment. It implies that when you first have to make something, or at least up until the point you 'make it', inappropriate or immoral conduct is permissible. And then you have the responsibility or conscience to 'give back', hiding and offsetting poor choices and negative impacts, such as supply chain abuse, slavery, and pollution, with donations. How we have abused the environment, the carefree attitude towards packaging, waste and single use plastic, is coming back to haunt us.

I believe success comes from doing the right thing, helping people, providing a service, changing the way people think, and that type of success far outstrips the temporary financial elevation achieved by short term profit led tactics. What I'm saying is that good business *is* being good right from the get go. Working ethically, driven by principles, conscious of people, the environment, and willing to support and help people, this is the way to real enduring and sustainable success.

Y-Vonne Hutchinson, founder of Ready Set, which operates as a consultancy adviser for large organisations in

Silicon Valley on diversity, discusses how for inclusivity to mean anything, it must be integrated into the organisation and its strategy from the get-go, rather than merely a bureaucratic afterthought. Her own business is exemplary of this. With the reality of sexual harassment, social injustice, and gender inequality thrown into starker and starker light, her company is helping tech giants correct their ideology and practices. This is not only a valiant effort to address a social issue that, no doubt, affects her on a personal level, it is also in line with the 2030 global goals set by the UN. The upside for the companies in question is not only creating a better public image and aligning with the increasing onus to rectify equality standards, but also practical: a tolerant and safe working environment is paramount for retaining top talent in the industry, especially as greater and greater numbers of the best people in tech are women or from a minority background. Ready Set stands up for women and minorities, addressing a significant social concern, whilst also doing business with some of the richest companies in the world. Morality and business sense are aligned here.

If you make something, or have a service, that genuinely improves people's lives, you will have people and organisations flocking to you. And sometimes, the best way to improve *everyone's* lives is to improve *one person's*.

For example, let's say you have a grandmother living in an old person's home. She is suffering from severe loneliness. With work and other commitments, you're not able to visit as often as you like. So, working with a programmer, you develop an AI app that interacts with grandma at least once a day. She can ask it questions and it will ask them in return. It registers her intonations to determine its next moves. It might even be able to pass on messages to your grandmother or show her pictures of the two of you in response to her reflections or comments.

You have created this app solely to help your grandmother, but now consider how widespread loneliness is. It is practically an epidemic in the modern world. *Over 9 million people in the UK profess to being frequently or always lonely*, which is roughly 20% of the population. The issue is far bigger than one person, and in creating this app, you unlock the potential to affect literal millions (not even taking into account the rest of the world).

Not only is it about identifying problems that currently trouble us, but it is also about predicting issues. It is not easy to do this. After all, since ancient times the ability to predict the future has been viewed with suspicion even by cultures that actively accepted and practised the art of divination. However, the more research we do into a field, the more likely we are able to detect stress points or concerns, whether it be an implicit threat, such as the looming antibiotic resistance in our population, or perhaps a target set by a governmental body, such as the 2030 UN agenda, which clearly sets out seventeen goals for us to globally meet. In the same way that we might identify a business opportunity, we can identify these upcoming challenges and seek to neutralise them before they become a problem.

In Japan, they are using machine-learning to boost English teaching in schools. This project precipitates a change in the national curriculum in two years that will require children from the age of 10 to learn English. AI robots can check the pronunciation of each student's English more accurately than many of the teachers. The education ministry is planning a pilot project costing around 250 million yen (US $227,000) to see whether it will make a difference. Not only do the robots talk fluidly (a far cry from the stuttering machine-speak we associate with text-to-voice automation) but they have physical bodies that can gesticulate, and digital eyes that show expressions, to aid in understanding.

Whilst this might seem to be an ambitious implementation, at a National level, if we truly consider the ramifications of this technology, it is much wider still. Might this technology be leveraged not only in developed countries such as Japan, but also in other countries where education is far more difficult or sometimes even actively oppressed? The fourth goal of the 2030 mandate is *quality education for all* – these robots could well improve learning in third world countries as well. It is, after all, almost certainly more cost effective than sending over scores of teachers every year.

Technology is not just for governments or large-scale corporations or organisations, it is for all of us, can be used and built-on and developed by all of us. It is as much about finding better uses of existing technologies as it is about creating new ones. This is the democratisation, the sixth and final 'D' of exponential technology. *Democratisation* is key to leveraging technology for good as it empowers people to find solutions, thus widening the knowledge base and technical abilities which can be drawn upon to address an issue. In previous eras of human history, it was very difficult for individuals with vast knowledge or expertise to pass on their wisdom to others. Thus, humanity retrograded as often as it stepped forward. The hygiene and innovation of Ancient Greece and Rome, which developed thermal baths, advanced metallurgy, and virtually peerless uranography, was quickly lost after the collapse of the Roman empire and the rise of a feudal world. Now, with information increasingly de-centralised and available to all, we can build upon the achievements of our contemporaries almost instantly.

A good example of this in practice is GUARDIUM. Mark Jeffery, Founder of Guardian Circle, has created a global 911 / 999 using the exponential technology of cryptocurrency. He was inspired to do so because of a harrowing personal experience that motivated him to address a problematic gap in emergency services. He revealed in a recent webinar that his wife had suffered what they thought, at the time, was a stroke. As she lay there, in the throes of pain, she knew she couldn't speak, thereby making the emergency service line useless, so she tried to text Mark a message asking for help. The message that came through to him was garbled as she struggled to type anything coherent, and Mark assumed it was just a pocket-text. He arrived home not too long after, realising with horror his mistake as he found his wife on the floor. He called an ambulance and she was rushed to hospital. Luckily, it was a severe migraine that had merely presented like a stroke. If it had been a real one, she would most certainly have died. After this traumatic event, they searched for an app that would allow the user to summon help at the press of a button, but none of them worked as they needed, simply ringing the police / emergency line. This would have been useless in their situation, as she was unable to talk. The more they researched the issue, the more Mark realised there was a gap here. It's estimated six billion people have no viable emergency number. Uber offer a faster response than the police in the majority of countries. In addition, police cannot trace your call if you ring from a mobile. To say this is outmoded is an understatement. He recognised that he needed to create something new, something that could allow people to summon real help at the push of a button.

Guardian Circle have created a universal phone app, GUARDIUM, that reaches out to a set list of contacts you decide upon (and you can even set it to reach out to other 'experts' in the area, such as an off-duty fireman, for example). It connects those people, shows them where they are on the map in relation to you, and allows them to form a strategy for help. It's empowering people to band together and solve problems that law enforcement can't. He also cited being inspired by the collective aid offered to areas affected by the hurricanes. Where the emergency services were too short staffed, everyday people banded together to create solutions, utilising what tools and resources they had to get people to safety.

It's time to stop demonising technology, fearing it as once sorcerers were feared by the monarchy, and start recognising the immense value it has to offer and good it can do in the hands of people with real values. If you are reading this and you feel inspired to make a change, to leverage technology for good, then I humbly encourage you to do just that. It's time to harness the powers available to us and transform the world we live in.

~

1.9 UN 2030 SDGs

In 2015, the UN established 17 Sustainable Development Goals for 2030. I view this in simple terms as the planet's 'to do' list. We have some issues, issues that we probably should have dealt with a long time ago, and now in some cases it's make or break, deal with them or risk entering a dystopian phase of humanity's existence. I've talked about the Big Grand Challenges we face and how we can leverage technology for good in the preceding chapters. The UN goals are a focal point for this, I think, as they provide some of the biggest challenges you could possibly face (literally global in scale) and meeting these challenges is certainly a way to leverage technology for good.

If you have never encountered the UN 2030 Sustainable Development Goals before, allow me to very briefly summarise. The SDGs are 17 objectives for building a sustainable future. They range from climate-related to societal and about improving the quality of life for many areas of the world. In creating a fixed deadline, doing away with wishy-washy sentiments and instead giving us a fixed target, the 2030 agenda is designed to motivate and inspire humanity to rally together and take on these issues in a serious and focused way. In many instances, if we do not fix these issues, we will cause irreparable damage to our planet and our fellow human beings.

The goals are: no poverty; zero hunger; good health and well-being; quality education; gender equality; clean water and sanitation; affordable and clean energy; decent work and economic growth; industry, innovation and infrastructure; reduced inequalities; sustainable cities and communities; responsible production and consumption; climate action; life below water; life on land; peace, justice and strong institutions; partnerships for the goals.

THE GLOBAL GOALS

Needless to say, these are incredibly ambitious! But, without ambition, without dreaming, it's impossible to create a better future.

There's a lot more information available on the UN website (*www.globalgoals.org*) and in other places for those of you who want to find out more and perhaps even begin working on these goals.

I want to tell you now how I first became aware of the goals and what they mean to me, because it may well inspire your own thinking and direction, and provide you with a wider context for the book you hold in your hands.

My first 'real' company was a Brand Communications agency, founded in 2000. We specialised in brand strategy, connected content campaigns, and marketing automation for many large and well-known brands for nearly two decades: from Sony Professional, Thomson Reuters, and Vodafone, to hundreds of challenger brands and start-ups over the 17 years before I sold the business in 2017. Starting, scaling, and exiting this business gifted me with a wonderful education, powerful network, and unique experiences. A gift I will forever be grateful for. Employing almost 100 talented team members over this period enabled me to acquire a number of unique capabilities and experiences, ones I continually leverage to build a bigger future.

In 2015, as a leadership team, we made the strategic decision to go for our first tender, our first bid, and went all out for a big one – one for a UN agency. Up until this point most of our large corporate clients came from our network, relationships, and a reputation built up over years of hard work and delivering against promises. With the help of our whole team, we put together the application, which was about as rigorous as one would expect to work for the UN. To be honest, we thought the process would get our paperwork in order for future tenders, part of each of us believing it was such a long shot we were unlikely to win against larger, more accomplished agencies from around the world. To our surprise and delight we secured a contract to drive the global rebrand and repositioning of United Nation Volunteers (UNV). This was one of the most incredible experiences of my life and career, and I'm eternally grateful for the opportunity; to the team, who committed way beyond the call of duty, inspiring each other to work on a project that truly matters, a life's work opportunity, if you will. And ultimately to the executives at UNV, who with some extensive persuasion were brave enough in their decision making to embrace our thinking, ideas, and vision for the future of their brand.

The challenge facing us was complex and multi-faceted. In part we were engaged

to help increase the international placement of volunteers across the UN estate, enrich the sense of pride felt by them, and generate a greater understanding and awareness of the important contribution volunteering makes towards sustainable development. In order to achieve this, we would need to simplify the complex messaging, engage emotionally with their audiences, unify and modernise their communication, and update their core identity to match who they are now and the place they want to own in the future.

The work took 14 months and was delivered in 12 phases. It involved everything from significant stakeholder research to the final brand positioning, strategy, and roll out. During this time, I personally funded a mission to Nairobi, Kenya, to get a deeper understanding of the work on the ground, to speak with real volunteers and see the challenges they faced and the difference they were making. I ran workshops across multiple agencies and gathered incredible insights to close the gap between the field and the centralise head office in Bonn. It was a humbling privilege I will never forget.

Following on from this work, I was invited to deliver a keynote speech in Vienna at the UN's annual Communication Group General Conference, where the most senior communications leaders and chiefs from every UN agency meet. The topic was the brand strategy of the Global Goals and shifting from surviving to thriving. As I approached the building in which the conference would be held, I remember quite distinctly thinking: 'This is my mark'. This is where I can begin, in a small way, to influence some leading organisations of the world. It was an eerie feeling, like walking onto a movie-set. I knew, however, I was here for a reason.

My concept was to take the room to the place of achievement, to 2030 where the goals were successfully met. I asked them: What role did they play? How did they inspire new ways of doing things? How might they need to let go of 'consistency' and rigid processes and embrace experimentation and an open-minded collaborations? What barriers did they need to break down, internally, with how communications were often overly complex, lengthy, and quite honestly boring, lacking a real emotional connection.

The truth is, my mind had been set on fire by the SDGs, the idea of making a difference to the planet. This was the mark I wanted to leave, how we must all embrace a rapid approach, to co-create with audiences and not to singularly govern and create from within.

For me it had become so much bigger than marketing as a serial entrepreneur. I was being drawn by the magnetism of these new and colossal challenges: world hunger, inequality, poverty, educational deficit, clean energy, housing, the decline of the natural world.

The best way of making a difference in those areas with my unique capabilities, however, was not directly, but indirectly. It was in facilitating and inspiring others already working towards these objectives to problem solve, to make significant innovative leaps, and to get there quicker. For this, and, in balance, I co-founded Leaps Innovation with one of my closest colleagues from my agency and friend, Mike Raven. Leaps is an organisation driven to helping companies drive breakthrough innovations, using rapid collaboration and methodologies to expand horizons and open up new solutions for companies futures. Together with Adaptai and a number of collaborations we are building the new operating system for change; a community transforming the way companies navigate the exponential future we face. My life has never been more purposeful, and my meaning has never been clearer.

Exercise:

Consider now how you might interact with the SDGs. Is this the first time you are hearing about them? Which draw you like a magnet? What issues do you care about more passionately than others. Consider what would inspire you for the next 25 years, giving you a continual source of inspiration and energy to build a bigger and better future?

~

1.10 Moonshot Innovation

A moonshot is not just a 'big goal'. If you were a psychologist, and you wanted to double the number of therapy sessions you could give in a year, that's big, it's admirable, but it's not a moonshot. Why? Because you probably know how to do it.

If you know how to do it, it's not a moonshot.

Moonshots are about expanding our thinking and stepping into the unknown. When President Kennedy said we would put a man on the moon, he admitted we didn't know how to do this yet, but that didn't shake his resolve that we were going to do it anyway. Moonshots are counter-intuitive, we almost have to think backwards to get to grips with them. We have to ask ourselves: What technology will exist or is likely to exist in twenty years time? Where are we now? Where can I find the intersection between that and the big challenge that we face in the next couple of years? Having a moonshot breakthrough comes from giving yourself permission to dream, to open up your imagination to crazy 'what ifs'. It is like being a child again.

One of the best ways I've found to get you in the right mindset, with a better sense of how moonshots work and how we can become moonshot thinkers, is by playing a game, tapping into that childish urge to create and experiment. There is a hard to find moonshots game from 'X', Google's company for moonshot. Here is a small example of how to play it: you'll need a few sheets of card, pen, and a lot of imagination!

- Select ten cards and mark them as 'problems'. Write down some of the world's biggest concerns: world hunger, poverty, inequality, war, bacterial resistance, any issue that resonates with you. Using the UN Global Goals is a good place to start.
- Now, select ten more cards and mark them as 'technologies'. Write down any crazy sci-fi technology you can think of. It could be hoverboards, spaceships, cloning, it doesn't have to be available to everyone now, let your imagination run riot.
- Shuffle the problems and shuffle the technologies and then draw one of each. You now have to come up with a way to use that technology to solve the problem on the card. Write down your solution in 50 or so words.

The results are unpredictable and a little crazy, as they should be! Let's look at an example. What if one of your problems was 'shortage of fossil fuels' and the solution you drew was 'spaceships'. For this, one solution might be 'using the spaceships to mine asteroids and other planets'. Another might be 'to construct economical spaceships (that don't run on fossils) and to replace current fossil-fuel based transportation'. You can now weigh both of these options. Maybe ask some friends which they think is better. You can make this into a full blown competition with some of your friends and colleagues if you like, and offer points or rewards for the best 'way out there' answers. Remember, bad ideas often lead to good ones. Don't censor yourself. Don't shoot down your ideas before you've even started. Anything goes, and sometimes the most radical ideas are the best solutions!

Another phrase for this might be 'tangential or lateral thinking'. Rather than approaching problems in the way they have always been approached, this game allows you to see that sometimes unexpected convergences can provide incredible breakthrough transformations.

I have mentioned previously that one of the key subdimensions of AQ (Adaptability Quotient) is Flexibility. Later in the book, we will be talking about Rapid Experimentation, which is one of the outcomes of a flexible mindset. These are essential skills for learning how to adapt in the exponential world of tomorrow. The great thing is that your ability to think flexibly (or "laterally") is not fixed or pre-determined, it can be improved. And playing the "moonshot game" is one way to develop it!

We're going to talk a little bit more in later chapters about developing the mindset of exponential leadership and how maintaining this mindset can help you achieve your moonshot goals. However, one of the key factors to introduce you to now that is paired with imagination is openness. In traditional thinking, if you wanted to accomplish something, you say: 'This is my idea, these are my resources. This is the scope of the project, this is what we have to work on to achieve it.' This is not moonshot thinking. Moonshot is saying: 'This is what I want to achieve, how might we do this?' and asking that question openly and to the entire world. Rather than fearfully guarding our projects and ambitions, we can share them. You will be surprised by how people will mobilise to help you and support what you're doing if they share your passion.

We discussed earlier the work of a true moonshot thinker and game changer: Steven Krein. Steven's business, **_StartUp Health_**, has been transforming the health sector, with remarkable impact in just eight years. Part of the way he has done this is by utterly embracing moonshot thinking. His company has outlined 11 Health Moonshots addressing 11 massive crises in the health sector that need to be dealt with, and invites startups to join their community, their army of health transformers, and contribute towards solving them.

These are the goals, to give you a sense of their scope:

1. *Access to Care Moonshot:* Together we can deliver quality care to everyone, regardless of location or income
2. *Cost to Zero Moonshot:* Together we can reduce the cost of care to "zero"
3. *Cure Disease Moonshot:* Together we can rid the world of disease

4. *Cancer Moonshot:* Together we can end cancer as we know it

5. *Women's Health Moonshot:* Together we can improve the health of every woman, closing the gender gap

6. *Children's Health Moonshot:* Together we can ensure that every child has access to quality care

7. *Nutrition & Fitness Moonshot:* Together we can ensure access to food, water, and a healthy lifestyle

8. *Brain Health Moonshot:* Together we can unlock the mysteries of the brain to improve health and wellness

9. *Mental Health & Happiness Moonshot:* Together we can connect mind, body, and spirit in the pursuit of wellbeing

10. *Longevity Moonshot:* Together we can add 50 healthy years to every human life

11. *Addiction Moonshot:* Together we can end addiction and the opioid epidemic

This has created a global tribe. With over 250 already inside and 20 making the grade every month, they are inspiring new start ups to not only join the conversation but work towards solving some of these moonshots. StartUp Health supports these efforts with amazing resources, coaching, advice, and funding. Can you see the power of this? By being open about the goals they want to achieve they have empowered and inspired others to bring their skills, passion, and resources to the table, vastly increasing the likelihood of these moonshots being met. Moonshots are personal but also unselfish. They are for the betterment of humanity. The more hands on deck, the better. You might have noticed every one of Steve Krein's moonshot definitions starts with the word 'together', and this is the heart of exponentialism. StartUp Health have created a miniature ecosystem with collaboration and mindset alignment at its heart. Consider how your moonshot might create its own ecosystem. Who will be drawn to your idea and share your passion, what kinds of people do you want to attract?

Part of moonshot thinking is 'falling in love with the problem, not the solution'. This is really important, because in order to solve big problems, you are going to have to try a lot of things that fail. You might have to completely re-think your approach (leverage Unlearning) if the technology isn't working or if the problem poses complications (such as there being new developments). At the same time, you are going to have to maintain high commitment and grit, with the dogged determination to keep you going through challenging times. This reflects the interactions between our AQ Character and our AQ Ability. Maintaining and developing the two is critical to success long term.

It's not easy. Knowing when you are fruitlessly pursuing a cul-de-sac, a dead end, and when you are simply in a dip that will lead to an upward curve later, is tricky. There is no patented formula for working it out. However, if you stay committed to the problem, not to a specific way you want to solve it, it will save you frustration and a sense of failure. To quote Arthur Conan Doyle, the creator of Sherlock Holmes: 'It is a capital mistake to theorize before one has data. Insensibly one begins to twist facts to suit theories, instead of theories to suit facts.'

We have this tendency, especially in the West. We become committed to an enterprise, a product, an idea, and then we try to bend reality to make it happen even when all the evidence shows us that it won't work, or maybe simply won't work in the massive way we want it to. We are passionate about the solution not the problem, so we make mistakes in how we go about solving that problem. Moonshot is about choosing to work on something seemingly impossible, but not about trying to butt our heads against the laws of the universe. It is a delicate balance finding that place in between. Look at it this way: How many companies can you think of that have become mired in a sunken costs fallacy where they keep releasing the same types of products, or they keep up the same crusty old processes, even though it has long been outmoded by new progress? I could name dozens, big names too, and their market share is falling all the time as a result. Bankruptcy is looming and I can tell you it happened slowly, then suddenly.

Naivety is looked down on in our modern corporate world, but naivety is the friend of the moonshot innovator. So many new start-ups fly in the face of conventions and are tremendously successful as a result. Naivety is oblivious to the doubts and social expectations that so often get in the way of our best ideas. In the coming chapters we'll be looking at some of these barriers in our thinking (and more literal obstacles) that get in the way of moonshots, and how we can overcome them. Part of this, of course, is the childlike mindset I mentioned, a mindset of imagination, playfulness, and fearlessness. It takes courage to think moonshot (and even more courage to *pursue* a moonshot), to hold your nerve and take the risk, but the rewards are not only tremendous, but exponentially healing too.

~

1.11 Barriers & Challenges for Innovation

"Our barriers and obstacles are the raw materials for innovation." -- Dan Sullivan.

There is an abundance of content already written on innovation and the barriers one might encounter in that process. I want to talk specifically about moonshot innovation and the kinds of obstacles people face when they are trying to shoot for the stars and the seemingly impossible.

Many traditional business models are based on scarcity. Value is derived from selling a product or service that is rare or in limited supply. However, exponential technologies are generating vast abundance in almost every possible field. So, one of the main barriers to overcome is re-thinking, or perhaps it is better described as *re-imagining*, the traditional business model. We have to Unlearn the old paradigm of thinking 'scarcity' and looking for what is in short supply, and instead look for what is in abundance. It goes to show *one of the biggest barriers is actually our past successes*. If something has worked one way for a long period of time, we can be reluctant to relinquish that process. Again, we're attached to the enterprise, the solution, and not the problem. However, to succeed in an exponential world, we must let go of previous models and embrace the new. We must learn how to 'unlearn'.

Let's look at a few examples of modern companies that have re-thought the traditional model with great success.

- Firstly, *Uber*. Uber have made a product a frictionless service. They have leveraged an abundance of cars owners who want the flexibility to earn income around their busy lives and people who need to make one-off journeys to provide a dramatically cheaper alternative taxi service. And this really is only scratching the surface of the potential in some ways. Uber, or a business model like it, might well provide the solution to our congested roadways and excessive pollution, as a potential future pivot will be made possible to move away from human drivers and leverage autonomous cars to act as travel-on-demand. Like software as a service, we will see TAAS, travel-as-a-service, with subscription-based and on-demand models, when the costs become 10X less than todays' Ubers. I mentioned in earlier chapters how making a difference to one person can ultimately lead to you making a difference to the whole world. In the same way, solving one problem can inadvertently lead to solving others, others that are in fact more grand in scale. The current car average utilisation is less than 4%, meaning for 96% of the time a car is simply parked. A future where this is 10X more efficient will transform city and urban transport, road sides and future smart city designs.

- *Airbnb*, like Uber, have leveraged the abundance of underutilised resources, in this case unused rooms. The timing was perfect, when many homeowners were looking to bring in extra income during an economic downturn. This in turn provided an alternative for travellers to stay in the spare rooms. Now giving rise to many small businesses for property owners, Airbnb allows people to rent an unused resource in order to encourage a sharing economy and cuts down on waste. This is linked to the democratisation that I've mentioned in previous chapters. Previously unused and inaccessible resources are being made available to everyone and shared thanks to a digital platform and mobile data services. Other sharing economy business models are driving innovations to reduce waste. Did you know the average run time of an electric drill is just 18 minutes, with almost every home having one. How many other tools and goods could we share, given better access? Tracking and platforms to enable membership-subscription libraries, giving access to way more than books. From spare rooms to fancy dress outfits, what are the items living dormant, in the dark cupboards around the world, which we could reimagine a more responsible way to manufacture and share at scale in a way technology is only now making this possible?

- *Ant Financial*, part of the Alibaba group, is one of many new, branchless digital banks. Like Monzo and Revolut, they have been able to leverage breakthroughs in technology to transform the customer experience of banking. Ant Financial, a 15 year old bank, has achieved a customer-centric service like no other, with small business loans approved within 2 seconds. Instant, automatic allocation of inactive capital. A minimum balance of just $0.14 kicks in wealth management services. They have zero branches and have amassed 700 million customers in 15 years. To put this in context, The Bank of America, a 96 year old institution, with over 4000 branches, take 20 days to approve a small business loan, don't have automatic allocation of inactive capital, and you need a $3 million balance to enable wealth management. And in 96 years of business have amassed 70 million customers, 10X less than Ant Financial have achieved.

With disruption in every sector, business models are ripe for reinvention. Now truly is the time for creativity, imagination, and bold ambitions.

These are just a few examples of how one can re-think the traditional business model and leverage the tremendous abundance of today's world. However, choosing a model is often the easiest part of introducing moonshot innovation to a team. The reality is that any time an organisation tries to transform itself, it will face opposition from within. It is no surprise, change can be very frightening for some people. I call this the 'Immune System Response' and we'll cover it in more detail in the next chapter.

Suffice to say, as the immune system in the company gets larger, it gets harder and harder for innovation to break through, which is why you have things like Skunk Works and separate sandboxes that don't have the same kind of governance, reporting lines, and responsibilities to show success at early stages. Keeping the current business model the same and running the transformative, innovative new model outside of it is one major way to overcome internal change-blockers and barriers to moonshots. In this way, you are beginning to create your own ecosystem, much like Facebook and Google, who run the start-ups they've purchased outside of the main organisation.

The first step is to learn, not to plan. For most companies, they go straight to the planning stage. 'Okay, what's the business model, what can we sell, how can we sell it, how can we make the product?' We like to repeat this mantra that failure is the key to success and if we get it wrong x number of times we'll eventually get it right. Yes and no. We want failure but actually what we want is to celebrate *learning*. Whenever we start to think about moonshot innovation, it's not thinking: 'We've got to build this and we're going to build it robustly.' Instead, we need to ask: 'What do we need to do first to learn something about this, not necessarily solve it?' We want to shift from failing slow to failing fast and failing forward. Learn through doing.

Learning Drive is another key sub-dimension of AQ Ability - and an important stepping stone to becoming adaptable. It also encomapsses our Unlearning ability. This topic is too rich for me to cover in detail within the scope of this book, so if you wish to find out more information on Learning Drive and also unlearning, you might want to visit *my free articles on Medium*. And do check out Barry O'Reilly's book *Unlearn*

We not only face barriers from within, our own inner doubts and fears of change, but also from outside. As Maxton said in my interview with him: 'Culture plays a significant role in restricting people and how they can excel.' He talked a lot about how the culture in India and also the Middle East is changing. Where once women and young people were often in oppressive environments, people are now starting to break through these cultural obstacles using technology and the abundance of information and interconnectivity in our world. I'm very aware, writing this, that I am still very lodged in my Western bias. Nairobi and my experience with the UN was really just a toe-dip into the wider world and only the beginning of that journey of understanding. However, one of the things that is becoming clearer and clearer is that the world is changing. Africa and certain parts of East Asia and other areas of the world, that were previously not as connected as we are, are going to be coming online very shortly. It's already happening. This means literal billions are going to suddenly have access to information, products, and services like never before. It also means we are going to start to see solutions coming out of places we never previously associated with those kinds of innovation: Uganda, Kenya, Kerala to name just a few.

I think one of the opportunities to dislodge these internal and external obstacles is self-belief and internally rising above them. This self-belief links to the key mindsets of exponential thinking and leadership, but it's interesting that often people who are not happy with the status quo, who want to change the game, are called 'disruptors'. For me, the term disruption has fair element of negativity around it. I think it is indicative of those trying to protect the status quo. So, I prefer to call them 'transformers'.

After all, we are not trying to disrupt our world, but transform it into something better and more beautiful. The ultimate barrier to our innovation is only ever ourselves.

Exercise:

Write down something that you wish to learn more about – it could be a technology, a process, a service – and then gather a list of resources together that could help you 'learn by doing'. Remember this important lesson: If you wanted to learn how to be a master-swordsman, a fencer, you couldn't learn that from a book! You have to do it.

Exercise:

Write down a list of potential barriers to innovation that you face, both internal and external. Reflect on this list through subsequent chapters, particularly 2.1 Exponential Leadership & 2.4 Working the Mindset Muscle.

~

1.12 Immune System Response

Our immune system is designed to keep us safe from biological threats. However, sometimes, our body can be 'disrupted' by a virus or toxin, or we make a drastic change to our lifestyle or diet, and then the immune system has trouble identifying what is helpful and what is an enemy. This is an auto-immune disorder. It causes your defensive white blood cells to attack *everything* and dramatically weakens the body, sometimes even fatally. Hair falls out. Skin turns bloody and is covered in awful rashes. Energy levels plummet. The body is fighting a war with itself. This is a truly terrible thing to happen to anybody and it happens not just at a personal biological level, but also at a psychological and an organisational level.

But why? Why do people resist the very changes which might just save them?

There is a tool called *Motivational Maps* which I have used both within my business and with some of my clients. It's a self-perception inventory that allows you to determine your true motivations and drivers (unlike a psychometric test which determines the 20% of your personality that is fixed due to biology and other immovable factors). The nine key motivators, which range from Defender (security) to Searcher (making a difference to others), are drawn from Maslow's Hierarchy of Needs, Edgar Schein's Career Anchors, and the Enneagram. According to the founder and creator, James Sale, we have all nine motivators within us, but they are ranked differently in each person, and they can change over time as we grow and develop. The nine motivators are divided into three 'clusters': Achievement, which is work-related; Relationship, which is people and family focused; and Growth, which is about personal development. This tool has revealed that those in the Relationship cluster, roughly 33% of the population, are actually predominantly past-orientated and change-averse. So, in your organisation, there are probably going to be a certain number of people, roughly 25 – 40% depending on the type of business you run and your recruitment methods, who fit into that category.

Please note that this is not necessarily a 'bad' thing. Process and security-driven people can be great in roles that require meticulous precision or repetition or fastidious checking. But prepare yourself for technological displacement as many of these tasks will be the first to find themselves automated and replaced. How people who are currently serving in these capacities transition and leverage another aspect of their makeup will be critical. Ensuring people feel part of a collective, with a future contribution to serve, will be an important social aspect of every ethical business. We need to commit to bringing all people with us, into this new technology driven world. However, they are not natural innovators and do not naturally seek moonshot innovation, viewing it as a threat to their security and well-being, hence they can, almost literally, 'attack'.

Further to this, the ways in which an organisation introduces innovation can often magnify the immune system problem. Innovation and R&D teams are commonly equipped to deliver value through efficiency and productivity. This is where the innovations of yesterday have borne reward, and further embedding behaviours aligned to these practices.

When it comes to cutting-edge innovation, to creating truly breakthrough ideas, organisations often recruit external consultants after trying and failing internally. To drive and achieve radical transformation can be antagonising to the teams employed to maintain and grow 'business-as-usual'. To be honest, unless careful preparation and fertile ground exists within an organisation, most will fail at this type of far horizon value creation. The freedom, trust, space and facilitation required is vastly underestimated. Asking your teams and people, who have been responsible to mitigate risk, to now take not a little, but a lot! To dream and give birth to crazy ideas is no simple behaviour and requires brain gymnastics even for the most creative in your teams.

Either way, the organisation's immune system will often attack any and all initiatives that don't look like previous successes.

To help neutralise a corporate immune system attack, have highly adaptable and experimental existing employees, separate from the core, and give them freedom, time and space to experiment. Remove the governance and reporting lines for approvals and allow autonomous execution. This will encourage the transformation process, which, alongside outside collaboration, might just develop your company's future lifeline.

Simultaneously, bring in measurement tools, platforms, and external coaches to psychologically and practically support your employees transition with adaptability. Transforming an organisation is not just about the organisation itself, but also about updating the mindset and knowledge base of the people who work for it so they are not 'left behind' by organisational change. You must transform your organisation's antibodies (its white cells) into highly adaptable champions – red blood cells dedicated to driving innovation.

One of the challenges with transformation processes is that either they are too long-winded so people lose interest (and the window of opportunity vanishes) or they are too flash-in-the-pan to truly shift the way people think, behave, and go about their business. I'd recommend a series of moonshot innovation design sprints, across a time-frame of 10 weeks, to kick-start the changes. It will challenge your organisation and push it, but providing the right support mechanisms are in place, it is achievable and has the potential to completely rewire what you do.

Changing the way people think, and the way you think,

is not easy. It is a painful sometimes torturous process that requires grit and determination. Figuring it out takes such a level of bravery and, I would argue, a sense of adventure. Shifting our thinking shifts our reality. The same event or process that makes somebody very stressful, very awkward, very uncomfortable, can be joyful for someone else with the right mindset. It's a *decision*. It's not the path you take but the mindset with which you take the path. You could set out on a big adventure and it be all about survival. Someone else could undertake the same adventure and it could be all about the experience and joy of what they did. The adventure is still the adventure.

And so I urge you in whatever adventure you undertake, whatever moonshot or transformation you aim for, to know that the adventure is not the reason why it's stressful and hard or why you are encountering huge seemingly un-scalable obstacles. It is your perspective and mindset that create them. If you, as a leader, do it with optimism, do it with joy, do it with excitement and effervescence, that becomes infectious. It is important to make sure you're infecting your surroundings, your employees, your work-space, your colleagues, your friends – infecting them with energy and vitality and excitement. Whilst I remain determined to create change in this world, I also recognise that there is no point achieving that change at the cost of all else. It's pointless to succeed in reaching a moonshot or a transformational goal, only to come out the other end near dead with exhaustion, stress, and a feeling of ill-will amongst the people you've been working with. To lose all of your emotional and physical resources and to kill the spirit of the team to get to the end is unhealthy and pretty unethical. Think about a marathon runner. Either you can get to the end happy, elated, feeling fitter than ever before, or you can drag yourself over the line against all the protestations of your body, refusing to listen to the warning signs it's sending you. One of these experiences leads to achievement and progress, the other perhaps to serious health problems later down the line for your business.

You want to arrive at that finish line with your energy and vitality still intact. Not only is this the best outcome for everyone, it's actually the best way to achieve the moonshot in the first place. When everyone is motivated, energised, and passionate, with purpose clearly aligned, you will harness the creative potential of those around you and benefit from the 'red blood cell' effect of organisational champions.

Tip:

Congratulations! You've reached the end of part one: Living in Exponential Times. By now, you probably have a good sense of what out world looks like, what it might look like in just a few years' time, and some of the opportunities that are going to be available. In the next section of the book, Exponential Leaders, we'll be looking at how we can leverage this exponential world, what the key attributes and mindsets of becoming a leader are, and 10x thinking.

~

PART 2:
EXPONENTIAL LEADERSHIP

~

2.1 Exponential Leaders of the Future

When we are in the womb, we are actually aware of our environment outside of it. Psychological studies have shown that the environment inhabited by a mother, and the corresponding effect it has on her, has a direct impact on the child. If the mother is relaxed and safe, the child is much more likely to be confident and assured. If the mother is constantly stressed and anxious, the child, even as it forms in the womb, will begin to prepare itself for the perceived dangers of the outside world, and is much more likely to develop an over-active amygdala, the part of the brain that deals with fight or flight and responding to danger. This can in turn lead to anxiety disorders or even panic-attacks, because in our modern world fighting or running are very rarely suitable solutions to the issues we face.

Just as we develop in the womb, each generation adapts to the world it is born into. How many times have you heard someone say: 'Kids these days, they don't even need to be shown how to use computers. They just know.' There's a grain of truth in this. Each generation is becoming more and more attuned to technology as our world increasingly fills up with computers, touch-screens, and mobile technology. However, even with this greater and greater affinity for tech, the reality is that most of us have still been brought up in a linear world with linear thinking. In the world of tomorrow, a world just around the corner, this thinking will no longer help us in the same way.

Our friend, The Futurist, thinks exponentially, and in some ways it is almost difficult to comprehend how that type of thinking works, the sheer scale and magnitude of it. But we must embrace it and try to comprehend it if we are to adapt to the new age. More than that, we need it to become the thought-leaders, the action-leaders of the future.

I have set the scene for you of what our world looks like and what it is likely going to look like. I have guided you through some of the grand challenges we face, and why we must adapt to the world of tomorrow. Now, I want to talk to you about how we do all of that. How we adapt, how we can help people in tomorrow's world, and how we create the future we want and deserve.

As with most things in life, it starts *internally*. What do I mean by that? Well, our thoughts are internal things we experience in our head that no one else can hear. Then, if we want, we can externalise them by speaking them out loud. Or, alternatively, by writing them down, drawing them, composing them, or sculpting them into a beautiful statue. Then, what is internal becomes external and visible to others. Michelangelo once said of his perhaps most famous statue,

David, 'I saw the angel in the marble and carved until I set him free.' I think this is a profound quote. He could visualise the statue waiting within the formless square block of marble. He merely set it free. Again, he made visible what was invisible. So, if we want to change the world and tackle big challenges, we must start with ourselves. We must change our thinking before we change what we do.

In order to do this, I have identified five unique attributes that define exponential leadership. If we are to become leaders and develop exponential thinking, we must embody these qualities and seek to manifest them in every facet of our lives.

Collaborative Innovator

An innovator is someone who introduces and fosters an environment for new methods, ideas, or products to thrive. Please note, this is not necessarily an inventor or someone who creates themselves, one doesn't have to be slaving away in a laboratory to be an innovator, but they are someone who facilitates the thirst for creation and problem solving by creating the right environment for it and encouraging others to bring their ideas to the table. A true innovator is seeking to embrace 'moonshot thinking' and drive breakthrough high impact value creation. The true innovator doesn't get frustrated when colleagues or employees bring them ideas for improving things, but views these interactions as opportunities to potentially improve an aspect of the organisation. Collaborative innovators also foster teamwork across diverse teams. When I say 'diverse', I mean not just in terms of background, age, ethnicity, but also skillset and values. These innovators can see the intersection between the various individuals in their teams and how they can best synergistically support one another. It's interesting that when considering AQ we define Environment as something that can 'help or inhibit adaption'. In other words, even the most adaptable people will find it harder to adapt if they are not being supported and facilitated. True Collaborative Innovators have the potential to boost the AQ of everyone around them!

Futurist

A futurist is someone who studies the future and makes predictions about it based on exponential and not linear thinking or current trend thinking. They have a deep understanding of linear versus exponential thinking. It is about looking forward, not necessarily with purely optimism, but looking with an exponential mindset in place. A good example of this can be found in the developers of Siri, the voice-activated virtual assistant. The developers of Siri knew when they were in development that the rest of the world was going to take two to three years to catch up. They were ahead of their time, looking to create something that could be integrated with the technology of the future, not the technology of now. Their foresight was vindicated, because they were bought by Apple once iOS had been developed. Siri is now an integral part of that brand.

Adaptable Experimenter

Traditionally, we look to the past for guidance. We look at previous research, data, and processes to determine what works and what doesn't. This is very useful for small-step increments, maybe gaining a 10% increase in customers or 15% more revenue in a year. When we think exponentially, however, we are looking for a 1000% increase in performance, a 1,000,000% upshot in impact or customers. We are thinking macro-logically, massively, on another scale entirely. To do this, we are going to have to embrace rapid experimentation and imagination (dreaming big which leads to big ideas). Being an adaptable experimenter is being continually open-minded to new methodologies for rapid validation and testing. It corresponds with the AQ sub-dimension of Flexibility. On a personal note, a lot of people believe they are open-minded, when in fact very few of us are. We default, much like computers, to certain models, behaviours, and procedures very quickly. However, to be adaptable experimenters, we must fight this urge to go with what is safe and embrace the strange, the weird, and serendipitous moments.

Technologist (BET)

The BET stands for Broad Exponential Technologist. In previous modes of thinking, a technologist would be someone who has vast amounts of knowledge in one specific area of technology. My views on leadership are not about having one area of specific knowledge, but more of a broader spectrum of awareness about what is out there, how it is being used, and where different technologies can intersect for common good. The magic is in the convergence of technologies.

Humanitarian

This is someone who seeks to promote human welfare, that puts people and planet at the heart of things. So, this sense of change, that is coming so, so quickly, is going to pull the rug out from under us. It's going to challenge our sense of identity, who we are, and what our purpose is on this planet. It's going to make us question ourselves and our roles in the age to come. We've talked a little bit about this earlier, but I can't stress enough just how challenging that is going to be on a psychological as well as practical level. We're already seeing a huge increase in suicides and mental health issues across the globe. Unfortunately, in present circumstances, I think this is only likely to increase. We need to make sure that we are aware of this issue and that people are not forgotten in our drive to develop. We are not building a technological world for the few, but for everyone. 'Leave no one behind' (indeed, my own company Adaptai is built on this principle, but more on that later). This is someone who embraces the SDGs, the Sustainable Development Goals, set out by the UN, and is an advocate for all life, human and animal.

Any one of these attributes is useful, but we are actually

looking for a blend of all five. Just as different exponential technologies interact and lead to breakthrough innovations, so too do these qualities compliment each other. In committing to these attributes, you are making your first steps toward becoming an exponential leader.

Three Horizon Thinking

Another important concept for exponential leadership is the Three Horizon Thinking framework. The idea is to prompt you to go beyond the traditional focus on innovation which is just in the present. This methodology helps us to move towards our desired future, as well as identify any potential disruptions which might occur as we move rapidly towards that future goal.

This first emerged in the 90s and it's been developed by a range of different practitioners, including the International Futures Forum, which I've worked with on several sustainable future development sessions. The approach can offer a way for connecting your innovation activities over these different horizons and how you manage what, in effect, is uncertainty in slightly different ways. It isn't a planning tool – it won't help you create a business proposition. It's a way of thinking about your business. Let me give an example to illustrate this.

So, the Three Horizons are H1, H2, and H3.

- H1 is about extending your core: the core services you have, the core products. This is about fine-tuning what is already there and optimising it. Often progress here comes through research and more traditional methods of developing a business. In other words 'linear thinking' works well here. This isn't about re-inventing the wheel, just finding better ways to do what you already do.

- H2 is looking at new builders to develop new opportunities. These are add-ons or extensions to the current product / service offering. So this is where you will see new software updates, new product updates that give you new features, or maybe even a replacement of an existing product with a new improved version. This is expanding your range and exploring those gaps in the market with related but new offerings.

- H3, which is the most difficult for every organization that I've met, is the visionary level. This is how we create viable options that are almost science fiction. This is really where the opportunity to piggyback on exponential technologies occurs. Horizon Three thinking will drive completely new products, services, business models, and ecosystems. This is where moonshot thinking takes place.

Another way to think of this is in the difference between kaizen and innovation. Kaizen is a Japanese word that literally means 'improvement'. However, it represents much more than this simple literal meaning. It ties in with the Taoist concept that 'A journey of a thousand miles begins with a single step', meaning that in order to reach our goal, we must make a multitude of tiny steps towards it (rather than trying to leap it in one go). This is H1, a process that requires those minute steps of adjustment. Note that H1 or linear thinking has its place, it is not to be abandoned entirely. However, for H2 and especially H3 thinking, we need innovation: bold leaps, moonshots.

So, we recommend that you design your innovation to span across the three horizons. However, bear in mind that it will take different teams and people to implement these and that the immune system response is going to make it harder across H2 and H3. H3 will likely radical your business and the current market you are in. You must remain aware of changes afoot (as any Futurist should) and ensure that nothing you are doing in H1 and H2 is about to become obsolete because of what you are doing in H3. Finding the balance between all three of these horizons is a sure key to success.

The Japanese airline ANA has sponsored the $22 million Avatar XPrize in order to do this in an incredibly counter-intuitive way. We might describe this almost as 'self-disruption', a transport company funding the creation of a special high-tech suit that will render traditional transportation, in some ways, obsolete. The prize furthers the development of a system that can digitally transport consciousness into a robotic body in a remote area where the user can physically impart skills and knowledge without having to travel. One would think that the airline is working against its own interests, but on the contrary, ANA is using technology to encourage new ways of travel thought impossible whilst achieving their MTP: connecting cultures and assisting humanity. Whilst they're at it, they're making the Sci-Fi movie Surrogates a reality.

Let's recap. The Five Attributes of an Exponential Leader are:

- Futurist
- Technologist   (BET)
- Collaborative Innovator
- Adaptable Experimenter
- Humanitarian.

~

2.2 The Power of an MTP

Tony Robbins once said: 'Emotion is what activates everything... Information without emotion is basically not held on to.' Throughout the course of this book, we've looked at a lot of information about exponential technologies and how they are changing the way we live. Hopefully, alongside that, you've also felt a little bit of emotion. Maybe you've been inspired by one particular story, or even frightened by just how rapid the advance of the future is. Whatever your reaction, I should make it clear, there's no point in trying to take on a Big Grand Challenge if fundamentally you don't feel passion for it or have some sort of emotional connection. Passion is the driver. Passion is what will push you to experiment, to keep going even when it seems like the solution is unobtainable. Even negative emotions can be powerful and useful. Do issues of social justice make you feel anger? Does the inequality of our modern world grind your gears? This anger can be a good thing, driving you to make a positive difference and change what you don't like in the world.

This passion, however, needs to be channelled and focused if it is to be correctly harnessed for moonshot thinking. This is where MTP comes in, or a Massive Transformational Purpose. If we just take a moment to think about those words, it's quite revealing. It's not just any purpose, it's 'massive'. It's on a grand scale. It's tackling those big grand challenges, those SDGs, thinking global rather than local. It's also 'transformational', or in other words, it's making a difference to people. The MTP is not a 'goal' however, it transcends a goal, it is eternal and feeds your goals. You do not pursue an MTP, it isn't an ultimate aim or end you can achieve. It instead is something which expands within you.

So, your MTP should be something which is clear and laser-precise, easily definable, a mantra you can repeat to yourself down the years and know it still has validity. Of course, this is not to say that your MTP cannot shift as you gain a better understanding of your field, or in direct response to changes in the world – one needs to embrace change as we described in the *8 mindsets* – but the root of it is the same.

Part of an MTP is circumnavigating the 'how'. This might sound counter-intuitive, especially, I think, to my colleagues in Britain where generally radicalism and ideological thinking is discouraged in the workplace. But this is exactly what you need to do. If the 'how' is the first thing you think of, most of the time you'll immediately stop, the difficulties and problems will scare you away from pursuing your ambition. Instead, your purpose and emotion should come first. This purpose and emotion will drive your creativity and innovation to solve the 'how'. My friend Dan Sullivan has so many quotable lines. Here is one of my favourites: 'Your eyes only see, and your ears only hear, what your brain is looking for.' I think this is rather profound. Have you ever noticed that once you become aware of something you begin to see it everywhere? You're introduced to a new actor you like and suddenly they're in every single movie you watch. Or you try out a new product and suddenly every billboard is advertising it. Of course, in our era of targeted advertising, it's not entirely down to the holographic coincidence of the universe, but our awareness plays a big part in picking up on these cues. So, when you have a clear MTP, which in turn will spawn clearly defined goals and parameters, you will begin to see things that can help you reach it. You will open your awareness, your sense of opportunity; suddenly, a random conversation with someone could lead to accomplishing something really profound.

The first step in identifying your MTP is to think about what your 'big grand challenge' is. Identify a problem area that resonates with emotion for you, whether that is anger, fear, wonder, or something even deeper. I am personally inspired and filled with wonder about technology, but I also have deep concern for those being left behind by the furious advance of technologisation. I wanted to pass on my passion to as many people as possible so that they are inspired to embrace change and make a difference in their own right. This was my grand challenge, to make sure no one is left behind, and to arm people with the tools to thrive in the new age that's coming.

The second step is to ask yourself: who do you want to be a hero to? This is about defining whose lives you want to transform. Tony Robbins said that: 'Either you've got to get around where it's better or where it's worse.' If you go to places where people are doing amazing things, it'll inspire you to want to be better and make a difference. If you go to where things are 'bad' – where there are social injustices, crimes, hunger, awful standards of living, that'll inspire you too in a different way. For me, the people I want to help are those who would otherwise be left behind by our exponential era. It's the people who want to adapt but do not know how. It's the business men and women who are caught like rabbits in the headlights of progress and know they need to do something but can't figure it out. This represents millions, maybe even billions, of livelihoods, and is where I feel I am best positioned to make a difference.

To define your MTP even further, a good exercise is to write down some action verbs that connect with your MTP. This is helping you to get clearer on what you want to do and achieve. Think about words that define you and your intentions, words that resonate across multiple 'yous' - by this I mean versions of yourself at different stages of your life. Do you think these action words will resonate with you in the future as well? Most people, when they really get deep into understanding themselves, they realise while so many things can change for us, and drastically change, there remains a core that is often carried throughout our lives.

For me, that core is making a difference. I think, deep down, I have always wanted to make a difference, and though it found expression in different types of businesses and activities, and through different stages of growth in my life, there was always this core. What is your core? Is it 'solve', 'change', 'inspire'?

I think it's time I shared with you my overarching MTP, it is:

to unite, inspire and accelerate the best of all humanity.

This is the summation of my philosophy and life's purpose. It is a part of my being, and, if the word is permissible, my soul. I think you will clearly be able to see the thread of this purpose running through this book.

It is okay to change your MTP as you change. It is also okay to have a few MTPs. Perhaps, like me, you have a number of businesses. And for each of them, there is one. For my business Adaptai, it is: 'to unlock the secrets of human adaptability, ensuring no one is left behind in the fastest period of change in history'. You can see how this feeds into my own personal one of uniting humanity. I have found discovering and articulating my own MTP to be hard, but tremendously rewarding and magnetic. Once shared, people either bounce out or deeply in; it is that black and white. The level of commitment and heartfelt dedication from our emerging teams is a blessing and honour to witness. When people are aligned in this way, working on something they consider part of their own 'life's work', motivation, productivity, creativity and outputs reach amazing new heights.

What is the thread of your purpose?

I'd like to invite you now to write down two to four different versions of your MTP. They should be similarly snappy and memorable (in fact, when you have chosen which one you want and which one connects most with you, you should memorise it). Contemplate them, search yourself, measure the emotional response you feel reading each one. There's no issue if you want to refine them a little more or tweak them slightly, but once you have settled on an MTP and the wording, try to internalise it.

For a lot of people I've spoken with, their MTP connects with something that they dreamed of being or doing as a child before the world told them 'no this isn't possible', 'this is unrealistic'. Challenge those doubtful 'hows' and unashamedly embrace the power of your true purpose.

Exercise:

Let's discover what your MTP is. Follow the four key steps.

1. *Identify your big grand challenge, one that resonates with emotion.*
2. *Ask yourself who you want to be a hero to, find your audience, the people you want to make a difference to.*
3. *Write down action verbs that connect with you.*
4. *Form several 20 – 30 word drafts of your MTP. Choose the one that resonates most.*

~

2.3 Preparing for Changes Ahead

I've said it before, but it's worth reiterating: we are approaching a period of change like no other in human history. We discussed in chapter 1.11 the massive 'disruption' that the first phase of Uber had in terms of allowing individuals to leverage the underutilized capacity of their own vehicles and take someone from A to B. Uber set themselves up with a new business model, making a product into a service, as a broker who provided the frictionless user experience, a simple tool in the middle, the connection between the person who needed something and the person who could provide it. This was made possible because of a number of exponential technologies; smartphones with dramatically increased processing power, fast wifi, and 3G and 4G data connections, plus simple and secure digital payment services.

But the change isn't going to stop there. We've got to be ready for the next phases; this is only the beginning. Uber are now shifting to autonomous vehicles, which is going to create even more 'disruption' (or should I say transformation) when the drivers are going to be displaced. Early 2018 they entered into an agreement with Volvo, ordering 24,000 autonomous XC90 SUVs to be delivered between 2019 and 2021. The Financial Times estimated the deal would be worth around $1.4 billion, with the XC90's consumer pricing at around $46,900 in the U.S.. Uber were already testing the XC90 in Arizona, San Francisco and Pittsburgh, with safety drivers on board to help improve their software. Just a few months later, Japanese carmaker Toyota signed a partnership agreement to invest $500m (£387m) in Uber to jointly develop self-driving cars. In August 2018 it was reported that Uber were sinking around $1m-$2m into its self-driving car efforts, so far without ideal results: one fatal crash, a lawsuit, and increasing pressure from the progress of competitors such as Waymo. As you can see, Uber are determined to prepare for the changes ahead, investing intensive time, research, and funds into making their dream a reality. I think it highly likely that personal car ownership will decline once self-driving cars become an everyday reality, and Uber and Toyota are going a long way to making this more sustainable future model possible.

However, not only is this an incredible business opportunity, but it is also going to be a dematerialisation and democratisation of travel. Perhaps the next transformation will be a new company owned by users on the blockchain and available to everyone as a decentralised version of Uber? In addition, all this time spent commuting is going to be opened up. Think about what this means to you, your current business, and how you might utilize that time with your audience in a different way? What are tomorrow's commuters going to do? Is it going to be used for learning, training and education? Is it going to be used for entertainment? What's going to be the new use of the time when people are travelling when it's taken care of by AI?

It's also happening above ground in terms of the convergence of drones and sensors to now look at electric-powered flying taxis. In January 2018, I shared a breakfast with Jeff Holden, the chief product officer running the 'Uber Elevate' program. The potential is significant, changing the nature of short commute distances in built up areas. Uber are aiming to begin roll out of their VTOL (vertical takeoff and landing) aircraft in Dallas, Los Angeles, and a to-be-announced international market, by 2023. It's just around the corner. The aim is not only to radically overhaul travel, but also to create quiet and environmentally conscious transportation network.

The first Uber Elevate test plan transported someone from LA airport to downtown in nine minutes, a trip which can take over 2 hours in rush hour. Believe me, I've sat in it! FAA estimates about 1.6 million drones flying by 2021. Being able to access areas previously very difficult to get to is going to change the way we think about international aid. Consider areas of conflict, such as Syria, areas where refugees need resources but roadblocks and borders prevent us. People that have been displaced, that need health care, that need food, that need first aid, they are no longer isolated in their country, but reachable. A lot of the challenge previously was 'how to get it there' and the logistics; drones are making giant leaps towards solving this grand challenge.

So, we need to start to embrace exponential technologies as our collaboration buddy, as our friend, as our partner, to start to think about how we can contribute and unlock opportunities within our organizations and businesses. How do we do more with less? Less can be defined as less time, less resources or money, or all of these things. In order to help you begin to think about how to do this, take a moment to look at the ten questions below and consider your answers and how this might change your focus and resources.

- How many experiments are you doing?
- Who might you collaborate with to take on a bigger challenge?
- How many new propositions are you testing and prototyping every month?
- Is your business model right for the future?
- Are you measuring the adaptability, the AQ of your new hires, your current team, and your whole organisation?
- What do you need to STOP doing? What do you need to let go of and unlearn?
- Are you investing in rapid learning and programs to expand your horizons?
- Where are your best chances for breakthroughs going to come from? Do you have a moonshot team, or a moonshot meetup?
- When might we benefit from investing in a CAO, Chief

Adaptability Officer

- **And very importantly, do you and your team have the right mindsets for innovation, innovation in an exponential age?**

Hopefully, your answers will have generated some insight for you about where you are, how prepared you might be, and where you could potentially go from here.

How do we make sure we're doing the right things and doing them well. In fact one of the best quotes which profoundly applies here is one of my favorite from Peter F. Drucker: "Efficiency is doing the thing right. Effectiveness is doing the right thing... There is nothing quite so useless as doing with great efficiency something that should not be done at all."

Normally, when I ask these questions on webinars or polls, just over 70% of people say they are doing five or less experiments / prototypes per year, so roughly one every couple of months.

What I want to take you through, over the next few chapters, is some of our methodologies for unlocking the benefits of rapid experimentation, to encourage you to experiment more, diversify your thinking, and finally to know where to pivot and where to focus and double down your resources.

I founded my company Leaps to solve this very problem and to help organisations prepare for the changes ahead, from our expanding your horizons in one day workshops on exponential technologies, to our deeper programs for generating and testing ideas at light speed. I'm proud of our contributions in transforming the way many organisations approach moonshot innovation. The name is based on a simple acronym:

Landscape
Envisage
Agree
Prototype
Screen

These core five phases form the basis of the framework and methodology. Whilst modular, when followed through in rapid succession, you are able to shift the mindsets and help teams rethink how to approach challenges, and how to encourage more radical experimentation and collaboration. Preparing for the changes ahead, if the outside world is accelerating, we better learn how to be faster inside our organisations. If we are to prepare ourselves for the reality that we haven't seen anything yet, then we must reimagine parts of our businesses in ways we would never have thought possible only last week.

"...here we must run as fast as we can, just to stay in place. And if you wish to go anywhere you must run twice as fast as that." - Lewis Carroll, Alice in Wonderland

It's taking things that are ideas and discovering how we can get those into physical or testable forms and then get them in front of the right individuals as soon as we can, to listen, learn, and observe. And it's about doing this really early on before you've made too many decisions. I'm not talking about traditional surveys and traditional market research but learning by doing, putting and sharing your hypothosises in the hands of your audience and directly observing as the creators. Not seeing this in a powerpoint report, but watching real people, with real reactions, feeling the disconnects and seeing the gaps, whilst identifying the energy and areas to explore further. Innovation is not an event. It's not something that you go to. It's not a place, a lab. Many organisations in the last decade or two, in an attempt to find the next breakthrough and attract diverse talent, have invested in 'innovation labs'. They put some bean bags in an unused space, get some nice things on the wall, and expect magic to happen. So many are funded for 2-3 years and then closed, shrunk or repurposed. Innovation is a tricky and often over-complicated process, but one without doubt enhanced with a long term commitment, the right mindset and stimulus, and a well defined purpose. And really, if we're talking about moonshot innovation in exponential times, it's about radically committed and brave small teams, given freedom to experiment that increases the propensity for massive breakthroughs.

~

2.4 Working Your Mindset Muscle

Even if you have cultivated all the right attributes: you're a futurist, technologist, collaborative innovator, adaptable experimenter and humanitarian, without the right mindset it is going to be very difficult for you to leverage value.

Imagine you are a boxer. You've trained every day for six months. You have a prize-winning physique and have worked out on the punchbag everyday until you're no longer able to lift your arms. None of this training, however, will mean anything if you go into the ring without the right mental attitude. An opponent much scrawnier and weaker than you will defeat you, because his mindset is the river upon which he can flow, able to capitalise on the minutest loss of focus with cunning, maneuverability, and ferocity. To put this another way, there is a Chinese proverb, which is: 'First is courage, second is strength, third is Kung Fu.' What this really means is that *mindset* comes first. Courage is first on the list. The inner strength and focus. Tenacity.

Next is strength. Your endurance and power. I like to think of this as your 'grit'. Lastly: Kung Fu, your skillset. Your skills and knowledge are, in some ways, the last in line of these important tri-factors.

Viewing this another way, we might correlate Courage, Strength & Kung Fu with the three core-dimensions of AQ. Courage is our AQ Ability (Our internal qualities we can develop such as Mindset and Resilience). AQ-Character is Strength (our Grit, Pro-Activity, Motivation Style - our ability to get through based on somewhat more fixed traits). Finally, Kung Fu is our AQ-Environment; the technical aspects of our workspace and support network.

I could go on giving examples, but I think you get the gist that the way we think is fundamental and has an almost disproportionate influence on the outcome of events. It's also worth noting that it's not only important for you to have the right mindset, but it is also going to be very difficult to leverage value across your team if they are also not on board. If key team members do not share this mindset then you are going to have a very, very tough time achieving your goals. Luckily, there are many ways to ensure unity within a team and to open discussions about our differences; one of these methods is to use a mindset scorecard.

Mindset is one of the core aspects of AQ Ability. As a result, we believe mindsets are a muscle. They are not fixed. They can be worked, trained even, and can change. At their heart, mindsets are a belief that determines how we respond to certain situations. These can be empowering, but can also trap us with defeatist thought loops. In 2006 at

Stanford University, Carol Dweck did research contrasting the difference between a fixed mindset and a growth mindset. The fixed mindset is just that, it is impaired by negative thought cycles and doubt. In basic terms the growth mindset is always looking to learn and change. Dweck has primary research interests in motivation, personality, and development. She teaches courses in Personality and Social Development as well as Motivation. Her key contribution to social psychology relates to implicit theories of intelligence, per her 2006 book *Mindset: The New Psychology of Success*. According to Dweck, individuals can be placed on a continuum according to their implicit views of where ability comes from. Some believe their success is based on innate ability; these are said to have a "fixed" theory of intelligence (fixed mindset). Others, who believe their success is based on hard work, learning, training and doggedness are said to have a "growth" or an "incremental" theory of intelligence (growth mindset). Individuals may not necessarily be aware of their own mindset, but their mindset can still be discerned based on their behavior. It is especially evident in their reaction to failure. Fixed-mindset individuals dread failure because it is a negative statement on their basic abilities, while growth mindset individuals don't mind or fear failure as much because they realize their performance can be improved and learning comes from failure. These two mindsets play an important role in all aspects of a person's life. Dweck argues that the growth mindset will allow a person to live a less stressful and more successful life. Dweck's definition of fixed and growth mindsets from a 2012 interview:

"In a fixed mindset students believe their basic abilities, their intelligence, their talents, are just fixed traits. They have a certain amount and that's that, and then their goal becomes to look smart all the time and never look dumb. In a growth mindset students understand that their talents and abilities can be developed through effort, good teaching and persistence. They don't necessarily think everyone's the same or anyone can be Einstein, but they believe everyone can get smarter if they work at it."

This is important because (1) individuals with a "growth" theory are more likely to continue working hard despite setbacks and (2) individuals' theories of intelligence can be affected by subtle environmental cues. For example, children given praise such as "good job, you're very smart" are much more likely to develop a fixed mindset, whereas if given compliments like "good job, you worked very hard" they are likely to develop a growth mindset. In other words, it is possible to encourage students, for example, to persist despite failure by encouraging them to think about learning in a certain way. When we talk about persisting despite failure, we of course are stepping into the realm of Resilience, a core aspect of AQ. The sub-dimensions are all interrelated and feed one another. A growth Mindset influences our ability to bounce back (resilience). Our ability to bounce back increases our impetus to learn (Learning Drive). And so on. To master AQ, we have to harness key mindsets.

Goal of mindset

Dweck's research challenges the common belief that intelligent people are born smart. But growth mindset is not just about hard work. Perhaps the most common misconception is simply equating the growth mindset with effort. "The growth mindset was intended to help close achievement gaps, not hide them. It is about telling the truth about a student's current achievement and then, together, doing something about it, helping him or her become smarter."

Practicing mindset

Dweck advises, "If parents want to give their children a gift, the best thing they can do is to teach their children to love challenges, be intrigued by mistakes, enjoy effort, and keep on learning. That way, their children don't have to be slaves of praise. They will have a lifelong way to build and repair their own confidence."

Dweck warns of the dangers of praising intelligence as it puts children in a fixed mindset, and they will not want to be challenged because they will not want to look stupid or make a mistake. She notes, "Praising children's intelligence harms motivation and it harms performance."

So, when founding Leaps Innovation I created my first mindset scorecard. These 8 mindsets for innovation and exponential leadership were defined at one of my quarterly workshops in Toronto, at Strategic Coach. I've been part of Strategic Coach for the last six years and they have a fabulous series of programs built for entrepreneurs (we'll talk more about these in chapter 2.5). At Leaps, we use these mindsets to underpin everything we do: who we hire, who we partner with, how we approach revelations in our sessions and the ways we examine company culture and breakthroughs in innovation. These mindsets are built to drive moonshot innovation.

The 8 Mindsets for Moonshot Innovation

1. Ambitious with a sense of global purpose

This is in many ways what we have been talking about in preceding chapters. It is a knowledge that the best is yet to come, a commitment to building a better future. This is the courage and grit to leave a positive legacy for humanity. I should say that many people can feel self-conscious when they talk about such big aims. They are embarrassed by ambition. This can also be due to the people you surround yourself with. Are they content with mediocrity? Do they just want things to stay the same as they always were because they are too scared of making a change? Surrounding yourself with like-minded people, people who share your drive to make a difference in the world, is a good way to get over the self-doubt that can creep in when you set your ambitions high.

2. Curious and always learning

This is a continual expansion of learning and knowledge.

It might be typified by an excitement at discovering new insights. Someone with this mindset wants to share and apply what they learn right away, rather than hoard knowledge to themselves where it can do little good for others. Being open to new information, that may contradict previous understandings, is important too. Reading that book by a competitor or a new voice in the field, going on that webinar for the first time, these are important steps to remaining open to new ideas and maintaining that curiosity. A thirst for knowledge will lead to insight which in turn can lead to breakthrough moments, whether that is in launching a new product, deepening a relationship, or restructuring your career or business.

3. Respectful and open

You believe that sharing information, ideas and knowledge results in greater success. Again, this idea of being open and transparent in all your dealings, this will encourage others around you to do the same and could lead to incredible opportunities and knowledge-shares. If you are open about your plans and ideas, you might well attract interest or be offered opportunities you wouldn't have had the chance to get involved with had you kept everything behind closed doors. Have you noticed that at every talk, there is always someone who asks a question that is not a question, it's just a statement so they can prove how much they know? Don't be that person! Value others and listen actively.

Truly embracing and practicing openness is hard, we have been rewarded in the past by scarcity, protecting knowledge, behind non-disclosure agreements. With large investments in R&D requiring legal protection to ensure a return on investment, a system by nature which does not promote open collaboration. In stark contrast we see true mavericks like Elon Musk open source and share their IP, research, development and innovations to aid the whole industry, a game changing advancement, for sure. Going against typical convention enables your 'competition' but only if you view the world as one in which we are all against one another.

4. Confident and decisive

You are measured and optimistic, you know when to make decisions and have confidence in your actions and your team around you. If you exude confidence, you will likely inspire your team with it too. Being decisive is important too because in our rapid era of accelerated change, indecision and procrastination is far worse than making the wrong decision. You can learn from wrong decisions and recover. If you hesitate and deliberate forever on an issue, the opportunity may well have flown you by. This is 'learn by doing' and stacking this with your 'experimental' mindset will unlock the marketplace and new data as your co-creators.

5. Experimental

In chapter 1.5 Adapt Like Never Before we discussed how we no longer have the time to spend 18 months developing a product before we put it to market. In order to succeed in an exponential era, you must get into the mindset of continually validating concepts, products and methods directly with the marketplace, in days and weeks, not months and years. This is an opportunity to innovate and try things out. It is about opening a dialogue with customers in a very direct and real way (again, the idea of being open and dealing honestly with people). By having things out there, you are opening yourself up to an open-feedback loop, which in turn creates learning opportunities. Learning lessons soon enough to course correct and pivot your thinking before it is too late is a vital aspect of experimentation. Who is the champion of experimentation in your organisation, who is de-risking your investments through continual testing and refinement?

6. Partnership

You serve and connect, driven by working in collaboration to achieve mutual success and growth. You inspire and unite the best in people. Becoming an exponential leader is not about beating down the competition and 'winning'. It is about working together with people to achieve mutual aims that benefit everyone. What can you gain from collaborating with others? Sharing knowledge? Probably a great deal! Great breakthroughs and moonshots are achieved when we operate in collaboration, small committed teams from diverse corners: from different industries, cultures, genders, ages, and of course don't forget to think of technology as one of your key collaborators too! We will soon see the power of collaborating with AI, often via voice, in problem solving and generative design as a normal way of creation. "Hey, Alexa, can you reshape bracket 462, between these two load bearing points, making it 20% lighter and from a more sustainable material?"

7. Investment and growth

You repeatedly invest your resources to discover new things and achieve greater impact, confident your inventiveness results in abundance. This is an important point. You have to invest your time, your energy, thinking, and yes, sometimes your money too. If you want to discover opportunities in the market, or places where people have need, or understand how new technologies could be applied in a different setting, then you have to invest, to discover, to experiment and learn more. Invest in innovation, invest in growth, invest in development on a new scale and build a better tomorrow. Or, risk collapse and irrelevance. Remember change happens slowly, very slowly, then suddenly, in the exponential world!

8. Embrace change

You are fully plugged-in to the fast changing world, you love to find new and better ways of doing things. You commit to new breakthroughs. There is an old-fashioned saying which is 'keep your ear close to the ground'. It has its origins in ancient tracking techniques where rangers could determine the direction of their quarry by hearing their steps reverberating through the ground. We use it now to mean: keep aware of what is going on around you. It is so important not just to seize upon one breakthrough and try to build a business around it, but to be constantly aware of new breakthroughs and embrace the change they bring.

Accompanying these is a mindset scorecard. The purpose of the scorecard is to gain an understanding of where you and others sit on the mindset spectrum, and to start a conversation. Where are there alignment issues, where are things working, how can we address any disparity in the team? Resolving issues and progressing with the same mindset will allow you and your team to fully leverage exponential technology. Where might there be alignments and gaps with your partners, your suppliers, your collaborators, your customers, your new recruits? Remember if you, like me, belief mindset is the foundation that all other actions flow from, how do you and will you measure this?

I'd actually like you to create your own scorecard, thinking about the mindsets that matter to you, to your future, to your team, company, industry. To help you, I have included the one created for Leaps innovation as an example. Complete this as a starting point of understanding. The scorecard has four statements associated with each mindset, and a rating on a scale of 1 - 12. Ratings 1 - 3 correspond with statement one; ratings 4 - 6 correspond with statement two; and so on. Read the statements carefully and think about which one most applies to where you are *now*. You will then have a choice to rate yourself according to which statement you feel aligned to.

For example, let's look at mindset number 8, Embrace Change. If you felt that the first statement: "You are fearful and risk-averse. You feel that everything you value is being threatened and destroyed" most applies to you, then you could rate yourself a 1 (this is absolutely true), 2 (this is fairly true but you are moving towards statement two), or 3 (you are somewhere between statements one and two). Hopefully, after reading this book, you do not fear change or fear that everything of value to you is being destroyed, but it is good to consider all possibilities.

Statement one (1 - 3) connects to statement three (7 - 9), and statement two (4 - 6) connects to statement four (10 - 12). They are separated by fear and success. Statement one is fearful of the new world that is coming and losing what they have. Statement three is not fearful, but they do not see value in 'trying new things' and adapting. An exponential leader needs to ideally have their mindset aligned with statements two and four. Statements one and three are change-resistant. It is not to say that somebody could not turn a statement one or three into a two or four and vastly change their outlook, but it is in my experience much, much more difficult to do. And, of course, the very nature of change resistant people is that they don't like change, so changing their 'fixed' mindset is harder than it is for most!

The important thing about this scorecard is not to feel any judgement from the results. It's okay if you are scared, or if you do "feel restricted by constant setbacks within your team." We all can feel trapped at times. However, the important action from this is to use it as a filter, who you align with and where you might focus your energy on improving your mindset muscle, getting to statement four. In the case of Embrace Change: "You are fully plugged-in to the fast changing world, you love to find new and better ways of doing things. You commit to new breakthroughs."

This scorecard system gives you a way to monitor your progress in different areas and act on improving your mindset. Rather than vaguely hoping to remain aligned with these values, you can check yourself against them and give yourself a rating out of 12. Where are you still lingering at a statement two? How can you turn that into a statement four?

As you have probably already guessed, thinking about these mindsets is not enough. Whilst it is important to align your thinking, this thinking also has to be manifested and put into practice.

To help you do this, I have identified 10 ways to spot the mindsets in action and shift behaviours.

- Firstly, embrace *"learn by doing"*. This new form of research is better suited for our current climate, the best way to learn is by doing. Or, if you prefer to think of it in this way, to learn kinaesthetically. One of the most common pieces of advice I hear content creators give is 'just start'. If you want to make a YouTube channel, just start. If you want to write a book, just start. If you spend years thinking about the best way to do it, not only will you never get around to it, but you'll probably also miss the boat. Start immediately. Yes, your first outputs will not be perfect, but you will learn through doing and improving. "If you are not uncomfortable about the launch, you have launched too late"

- Second, *say goodbye to location based talent wars, and hello to the crowd, digital nomads and a super engaged remote workforce.* Defining and sharing your MTP and your moonshot is incredibly magnetic, use it to attract and retain previously inaccessible talent. At Adaptai, we have people working all across the world, from programmers to product managers to researchers. We are entering a globally connected era, where 3 billion new minds will be online in the next few years. Prepare and open your processes to get the best people for the job, where-ever they may choose to live. This is the idea of thinking big and thinking globally. Let go of being a sheriff in a small town, and welcome yourself to running a global rapid response unit. Next we will be saying hello to digital twins, artificial intelligence that will hold jobs previously held by humans. They will 'sit' in the chairs of those now replaced and augment the decision-making for managers and earn seats at board tables. They might take different physical forms, from simple 'voice avatar' interfaces to convergences with robotics to look more like us. With artificial skin and seamless interactions. Enter the Westworld!

- Thirdly, *shift from being IP protective to being open source*. At Leaps, we are open source. We share our scorecards, our innovation, and the results of all the work we do.   In our digital age, it is becoming harder and harder to prevent information leaks anyway, so why not embrace the greater benefits of sharing and collaborating. The benefits of sharing expertise and data cannot be overstated. Think back to the neolithic period. Humans at this point were effectively cave-dwellers. They had vocal language but barely any system of writing. Most newborns would die before they reached the age of 3. The only way knowledge could be disseminated was through cave-drawings, which were a limited form of communication, and verbally passing it on to someone else. If you, for example, discovered how fire works – let's say you observe a spark from flint and tinder – you could only pass that on to your immediate circle, but no further. If they died, that information would be lost. The likelihood, too, that one of them could take your knowledge and further develop it, let's say by adding oil and rags to create torches and a more reliable light and heat source, is slim at best. This is why progress was slow then (although, we must be fair, progress of any kind was miraculous). Although today we live in what is undoubtedly the era of most rapid progress in human history, it's worth noting that Mesopotamian society developed at an alarming rate. We can only assume that the innovation of cuneiform, the earliest written language we are aware of, meant that the ease with which knowledge could now be shared led to exponential development. Within a few thousand years, human kind suddenly had agriculture, cities, religion, philosophy and even brain-surgery (skulls with metal plates to replace damaged sections have been discovered in the ruins of Uruk, the Sumerian capital). This just goes to show how sharing, and having a shared language, accelerates progress exponentially.

- Fourth, *move away from departmental silos and towards collaboration.* Again, we have a tendency to partition our business into constituent parts: accounting, marketing, sales, development, and these parts can often end up becoming very disjointed and even resentful of one another (almost seeing each other as competition). In fact, your business departments should be working together and sharing knowledge. This approach enhances connection, culture and innovation performance. But this is only a first step, to survive and thrive in the accelerated world I urge you to do more than this: to shift your collaboration thinking from your own departmental silos, beyond your suppliers, beyond your location or industry, and to those who share your overarching mission. Think of

Startup Health and Steve, bringing a community and ecosystem together to form a powerful collaborative army of transformers.

- Fifth – this one is simple – *move from rigid to fluid.* Adapt, change, go with the flow. If you are midway through the development of something and a recent scientific breakthrough challenges your project, don't make the mistake of blundering on. Re-adjust and work on it in a new way. In my view, to increase the success of moonshots and breakthrough innovation, this is critical. Leave the structure for your business as usual, your core. Removing the barriers and normal reporting during the 'make it up' phase. Then flow swiftly to the 'make it real'; 'rigid' thinking is often the catalyst for the 'make it recur' phase.

- Sixth, *focus less on status and more on what contribution you are making.* How much of our self-identity, meaning, and worth is tied up in our job role and title? This drives behaviour to strive for this external validation and peer positioning our whole lives. Value yourself not by whether you are a CEO or Director, but by the contribution you make each day, how you show up, the way you think and how you positively influence others to build positive mindsets. Consider this principle in relation to others too. Does this new potential business partner have all the right jargon and titles but actually very little to show in terms of how they have contributed to their industry and society as a whole?

- Seventh, *measure and reward success less by time and effort and more by results.* This is the simple view of two economies; the 'time and effort' and the 'risk and reward'. This can also be defined as the difference between the employee and entrepreneur worlds. How might you consider a shift away from driving efficiency to driving effectiveness and outcome? Yes, we all need to be efficient to some extent. If we are working in a laborious and onerous way that is impeding progress, we obviously need to consider changing this up (and often technology can help us do that). However, being effective is now more important than ever. Again, we live this principle at Adaptai. I like people who focus on results. Their methods might be esoteric, they might be getting results quicker than I really anticipated, but this is a valuable learning opportunity. I don't assume, if someone can achieve something faster than I can, that they must be doing it wrong. Maybe they are doing it right and I can learn from them. Ask yourself 'who' not 'how' and structure your reward to outcomes and learning.

- Eight, *shift from maintaining stability to pro-actively driving change.* In a linear world this approach has rewarded us. We have confidence from past success, which is valuable. However, as we enter the disruptive phase of exponential technologies we need a new navigator, a new approach. Remember this applies to your innovation, the innovation of tomorrow. For many it will help ensure you have a tomorrow! Know it takes a very different mindset and team to maintain stability than to drive change, asking either to perform the opposite task is like asking a fish to climb a tree.

Consider instead committing to change, identifying those within your team where this is a unique ability: those who envision new ways of doing things and embrace this fluctuation. Drive change through these champions, release their shackles and your breakthroughs might just yield fruit.

- Nine. *Don't 'manage' risk, optimise it.* Don't try and mitigate risks, all great innovations and leaps forward require them. A simple shift in words can have a dramatic domino effect on your thinking, culture and output. From 'manage' to 'optimise'; from control and fear, to flow and positivity. Build a place, an environment, a culture where it is encouraged to take risks. Take a chance and invest in new ideas. See where they lead, fast. This is the attribute of the Innovator we discussed in chapter 2.1. The innovator creates an environment where creativity and improvement is encouraged. This involves risk, risk of the unknown. It can't be avoided, so we must unlearn our relationship with risk. The best way to optimise risk is to shift your thinking, communicate clearly what uncertainty, what predictions, which hypothesis you want to gain data from. In a world where the ground is in constant motion, optimising your flow and processes to be as informed as you possibly can as to what is coming on the horizon is a valuable role. Who will be your chief of adaptability? Who will be your technology scout, your futurist? Of course, there is a health and safety issue, but I love the tongue in cheek T-shirts of the innovators in a well known top 5 global brand with the slogan "Health and safety third".

- Ten. Linked to the previous point, we must *move away from governance and control (of resources, employees) towards freedom and rapid experimentation.* Of course, this doesn't mean complete aimlessness. Use your MTP, your moonshot and the mindset scorecard to align your goals across the company. Then, once you have this new level of clarity, you can release your team. Gift your people the freedom to pursue these aims within their own unique ability. This will allow people to think laterally about improving aspects of the company and making progress. Many companies I have worked within over the past two decades are obsessed by the idea of control, rigidly implementing policies requiring super high levels of justification with an unclear, drawn out decision making process. In fact many don't even know how they make decisions, I find this remarkable. These structures are, seemingly, designed to crush any chances of true breakthrough innovation. It's time for this rigid, hierarchical, command and control style narrative to be relegated to the minority. It might still be suitable for specific areas of the emergency services and the army, but for tomorrow's businesses, it really has no place.

Bonus tip - *Follow this simple but profoundly impactful approach to getting things done.*

OPTIMISE - AUTOMATE - OUTSOURCE.

I first heard of this approach at a summit in Chicago. It was outlined by Ari Meisel, who describes himself as an, "Overwhelmologist". He helps entrepreneurs who have opportunities in excess of what their infrastructure can support to Optimize, Automate, and Outsource darn near everything. Thinking of this as a continual cyclic activity is helpful. Every 90 days review everything you do and see how it can be optimized, automated or outsourced. What you once outsourced, or even worse did yourself, might now be redundant with optimisation and technology to automate. For example, dictating notes for a secretary to type up was once standard practice to be more effective and efficient. Technology moved this from face-to-face dictation, to a recorder, then directly dictating to a computer via Dragon or some other speech-to-text service. At first, with questionable results and long training and a very unnatural speaking flow, to near perfect real time text translation on a smartphone. Great for short text style notes, less so for large bulky content. I remember, when I first got a livescribe pen for Christmas over 10 years ago: the faces of amazement when I showed colleagues the magic of linking audio recordings taken by the pen to your handwritten notes via a special paper. You could then search, playback your recordings, and even add cool animations to your notes. It shifted how I optimised my daily working and meetings. I then began to use services like Rev.com where my audio files could be transcribed at a $1 a minute by distributed humans, turned around in a day, or, if you were lucky, a few hours. Later on, it was $0.10 a minute for AI to do this almost instantly, a 10x cost saving, though with some early quality issues. I am now using a magical service, an audio-to-text platform with 600 minutes free per month of real time, highly accurate transcription, called otter.ai. Check it out and see how quickly this can automate additional content creation for your meetings, podcasts, and videos.

Let's recap:

The Eight Mindsets for Moonshot Innovation are:
1. *ambitious with a sense of global purpose,*
2. *curious and always learning,*
3. *respectful and open,*
4. *confident and decisive,*
5. *experimental,*

6. partnership,

7. investment and growth, &

8. embrace change.

How can you embody and maintain these mindsets in your day to day life?

~

2.5 Rapid Experimentation

What I'm proposing is really two things, a 'new' model for accelerated innovation combined with leveraging the power of a much bigger, more ambitious goal - a moonshot. I say 'new' but there is some degree of truth in the old proverb: 'There's nothing new under the sun.' All things have a beginning somewhere. I must give thanks to Jake Knapp and his book *Sprint*, published in 2016, which inspired the convergence of a decade of running and leading workshops, so many tools, assets and methodologies I had created, to bring creativity, problem solving, and effective collaboration within teams. It gave me a lot of direction for the framework underpinning many of our programs. The strap-line of Sprint is: *How To Solve Big Problems and Test New Ideas in Just Five Days*. I think this epitomises the rapid experimentation approach. Taking influence from this, and 17 years of running my brand and marketing agency, helped me to develop my own model for Leaps.

So, you probably have a sense now of why we need

to rapidly experiment (rather than taking months and years). With the pace of our world ever-increasing, we must increase the speed with which we can test new ideas and solutions. The beauty of an experiment is the simple notion of forming a hypothesis. By which I mean you don't know what the answer is going to be (unless, of course, you are manipulating your test to force the results to confirm your conclusion). Experimenting is showing a willingness to discover an answer. Interestingly the word experiment comes from the Latin 'experiri' which means simply 'to try'. I think that is deeply resonant.

Experiments are not just scientific in the literal sense, of course. We can experiment with new business models, new products, new collaborations.

Some of the most radical rapid experimentation we've being seeing recently is in the video-game / entertainment industry. Epic Games, a long established gaming company that has produced a multitude of iconic and cutting-edge titles, including the gritty Sci-Fi grimdark shooter *Gears of War*, has now reached a $15 billion valuation. It's most recent release, the viral global phenomenon *Fortnite*, currently has 200 million players engaged, a staggering number that supersedes pretty much any game in history and even the number of people currently subscribed to Netflix! What is most startling about this, however, is that the original *Fortnite* was modelled on a different set of mechanics and objectives: a zombie-survival game in which players had to survive waves of attacks whilst constructing defences and barricades. Hence the 'Fort' in the title. However, Epic

Games quickly perceived this wasn't working, that they were rapidly losing players, and knew they had to experiment with new game-modes and mechanics to resurrect the game and catapult it to the level of success they wanted to achieve.

Looking at other key players in the field, Epic quickly pivoted and re-designed *Fortnite* as a 'Battle Royale' experience, a game-type named after the Japanese movie, in which a group of combatants are placed in an arena and forced to fight down to one remaining champion. There was only one existing precedent for this: *Player Unknown Battlegrounds* (PUBG), which had been released earlier in 2017. PUBG, whilst successful, was riddled with issues. Epic Games saw the success of PUBG, but also how it could be improved, and took on the Battle Royale mechanic, effortlessly incorporating it into their gameplay system with a few clever tweaks and personal touches. Now, *Fortnite* is most known for its Battle Royale gameplay, and is seen as a key trend-setter in the industry. Top YouTubers, pockets of the twitterati, and Pro-Gamers stream *Fortnite* to millions of viewers daily.

Rather than stubbornly persisting with the same ideas, Epic Games rapidly adapted to the market and experimented in real-time, perceiving a trend before it had even fully become one. Battle Royale is now one of the most popular video-game genres out there. The February 2019 released *Apex Legends* marks a further significant entry in the genre, with over 10 million players on day one of release.

Epic Games looked to the future, as well as other game-changers, and rapidly experimented with their game in order to improve it. They learned what players liked and didn't like, took this on board, and have created what is probably the most profitable video-game in history. Epic were able to recognise that the market had entered a period of change, where gamers (consumers) were looking for something different.

In periods of change, there is a greater degree of uncertainty, so in some ways, we simply have to experiment, because we do not know what the future is going to hold. Uncertainty breeds fear, but if we can transcend that fear, it breeds opportunity. The English poet John Keats talked about 'negative capability' as a sign of genius. It is the degree to which a person can cope with ambiguity and uncertainty. Of course, in poetry, the aim is not to be scientifically exact, but to play with double-meaning, symbolic meaning, hidden subtext, and evoke emotional and spiritual responses in the reader.

To become exponential leaders, we must harness some of this poetic sensibility. Rather than wanting everything – our jobs, products, future prospects – to be clear-cut and one-way, we must instead look to make ourselves more fluid in pursuit of our immovable objectives. This is part of being committed to the problem and not the solution. The solution can change when we have negative capability and can switch our position without having to completely re-wire our brains, but the problem and our focus on it remains the same.

Let us look at this another way. In the past, I've talked and written articles about how we need more unreasonable people in business. What do I mean by that? I mean that we have to be unreasonable in order to reach the ever increasing demand for rapid innovation. If we are not, if we duly accept the status quo like sheep, we will never create those breakthroughs. As George Bernard Shaw puts it: "The reasonable man adapts himself to the world; the unreasonable one persists in trying to adapt the world to himself. Therefore, all progress depends on the unreasonable man."

It is interesting that in the last few years there has been a surge in the ever-growing array of problem-solving methods, tools, frameworks, and consultants. This ranges from methodologies like design thinking, to systems such as agile, sprints of all stripes, and lean techniques. Each has strengths and merits, and they can be powerful tools when used with intention. However, I've noticed that most of the time when they are adopted they become the focus of the team, often at the expense of the outcome.

In the extreme, I've heard stories about entire corporations brought down by agile worship. In these institutions it becomes almost cult-like, a religious devotion to the 'process' without any consideration of impact on the end-user, efficacy, or results. This kind of mindset is harmful and depleting. Rather than seeing the SCRUM — or whatever it may be—as a tool it's often seen as an end-goal itself. Completing a meeting becomes the objective, rather than using that particular meeting to meet the purpose and grander ambition. This kind of attitude is, in the long run, toxic. It becomes a kind of invasive yet invisible barrier to innovation.

So, how can we avoid this?

It's time for me to introduce you to 10x thinking and go deeper on the Leaps model.

~

2.6 Breakthrough & 10x Thinking

How do you know what a good idea looks like? Which should you back? These are the difficult questions that businesses and innovators battle with every day. In our accelerating world, we no longer have time to spend months contemplating our options, we have to act and to learn as we go. Exponential progress, as the Futurist described, is a series of doublings. Rather than thirty steps taking us thirty meters, instead, thirty steps will take us around the Earth twenty-six times. The difference in scale of these two numbers is almost incomprehensible. Looking at it in terms of computational power, which is a big driver of exponential technology, in 2010 a $1,000 laptop could make 10 billion calculations per second, roughly the equivalent of a mouse brain (and greater than the entire computational power of NASA when they went to the moon). It's estimated by 2023, a $1,000 laptop will be able to make 10 billion *billion* calculations in a second, the equivalent of a *human* brain. By 2049, the computational power of a $1,000 computer will be equivalent to the brain function of the entire human race. This model, and examples created by Ray Kurzweil, is where we need to be at when we think about our business. Not a 10% increase, but a 10x increase. Not thirty steps, but thirty doublings.

I've been working with Dan Sullivan from Strategic Coach for over 6 years now, first in their Signature program, then 10x, and now part of the very first Free Zone Frontier program. Getting to grips with your 10x ambition starts with a workshop day. This is essential. It's about creating an extraordinary environment for the accomplished entrepreneur looking to fast-track their big moonshot goals. It's for the ultra-focused individual who wants to work on their aims right now and has the means to get started. Why is this important? The reality is that going 10x can't be done alone. You need your team and those people around you. One of the key AQ-Environment measures is Community. What is your support-network like? And this isn't just people in your business. You need other like-minded entrepreneurs who are not part of your business. Most people, when they come to the 10x program, realise that they actually don't have many other people like this in their life. Organisations are now arising with the specific aim of putting like minded entrepreneurial leaders together via a connected network.

One of the key personal breakthroughs for me was understanding what to let go of in order to grow 10X, what to *stop* doing. This included anything that was not squarely placed in my unique ability, plus the realisation that the business model my agency was built on needed radical changes or else I needed to divest my energy to pastures new. This ultimately led to the sale of the agency in Dec 2017.

Think of something a little more historic: writing collectives. Many of the greatest writers in our time belong to a group where they could share their work with others, get feedback, generate ideas, spur each other on. The Bronte Sisters, the King family, The Inklings, which included C. S. Lewis, J. R. R. Tolkien and Charles Williams, among others. These spaces are extremely important for top level leaders and creators. Remember the mindset of partnership and open source?

Within Strategic Coach, one of the key focuses of their workshops is on building and effectively leading your version of a Self-Managing Company®, with an emphasis on exponential doublings or 'multiplying'. While you learn how to multiply what you do, your team will learn to multiply everything else that's needed to reach your goals. Part of this is alignment, which we talked about in relation to the mindsets. It's about getting everyone involved on board and excited about your future vision and maintaining that excitement throughout with well communicated and clear strategies.

Picture this: one day every quarter you step away from your business. During this time, you shift the focus from your company and the day-to-day running of things to you and your biggest ideas and objectives. Imagine what you could do with the space to think these things through. Big moonshot innovations require a lot of thought behind them, and while I'm an advocate of action and learning by doing, it all starts with a thought, a dream and thinking about our thinking.

One of the ways in which you can ensure you are thinking big, thinking 10X, is to release yourself from thinking you and your team have to solve the problem. Do not tame your ambitions based on the resources you have today, on the technology and network you know today, that you can access today, and instead look to where the puck *will* be, not where it is. This requires a degree of 'negative capability' and being comfortable with ambiguity, key skills that correspond with AQ.

Consider how you might leverage the crowd, not in raising funds, or gaining pre-sales through kickstarter, but to *solve* your moonshot. It's an escalation of the 'who' not 'how' approach I described earlier. Draw on the untapped resource that is billions of human minds! There are many platforms for doing this, including sites like **www.herox.com**, which allows you to upload your challenge and mobilise the entire planet to solve this through an incentive prize led model. This completely de-risks your investment as you only pay out when your challenge has been met. But you must ask yourself the question is it the problem being solved that I care about, or building the solution to it yourself?

This feedback should steer you towards what the optimum way for you to make a difference is, and how you might begin to look at solving problems. Remember, 10x thinking, exponential thinking, is about asking yourself not 'how can I get another fifty miles to the gallon' but 'how can I get another five thousand miles to the gallon'. If you have problems you want to solve, you have to start asking yourself impossible questions, and realising that the impossible is only defined by a moment in time. Four hundred years ago we might have thought it impossible to get to the moon. We now know this is possible because we have done it. So, what are the 'impossible' challenges in your business, or what do you want to achieve that seems so far-fetched it is almost science fiction? Ask these questions, throw them out in the universe, and see what answers come your way. The power of something as small as an apostrophe can change the entire meaning and paradigm, from impossible to i'mpossible

The old excuses we gave ourselves no longer apply. In our current day and age, funding is no longer purely in the hands of big investors but now available to everyone with a good idea - through the creation of crowd-funding. Anyone who has an understanding of Kickstarter or IndieGoGo or any of the other innumerable platforms emerging can get access to the largest pool of funding of all – the entirety of the online population. Crowdfunding is expected to reach $300 billion by the year 2025. Wherever you are on the planet, if you're connected, you can get capital with a good idea. This is the democratisation (remember the 6Ds of exponentials!) level, where people can now control what is made and what is backed.

To understand what 10x is about, let's look at a recent altruistic example. The XPRIZE is a nonprofit organisation with the aim of solving the grandest of challenges humanity faces, propelling innovation, using gamification, crowdsourcing, and incentives to bring about radical breakthroughs. Founded by Peter Diamandis, with its roots in a private space flight prize, you can now find many challenges, including the Global Learning XPRIZE, where teams from around the world compete to develop open source and scalable software that enables children ages seven to ten in developing countries to learn basic reading, writing, and arithmetic without adult assistance. Hundreds of teams from over 40 countries registered to compete, and last year, five finalists were selected. Elon Musk, Tesla and SpaceX Chief, provided $15 million to the Global Learning XPRIZE in September 2018 to help incentivise teams in the development of methods to reach 250 million children who do not have access to primary or secondary education and give them the means to self-teach reading, writing, and arithmetic, all within 15 months. Illiteracy is a huge and still widespread problem in the world (this is certainly a Big Grand Challenge and corresponds with the UN SDGs). Arguably, illiteracy precludes people from society to an even greater extent now our world is globally connected than it did pre-global interconnectivity. The wealth of opportunity for people who have access to the internet and can read cannot be overstated. Entire businesses arise from social media interactions and content sharing.

While programs already exist to build schools and train teachers, they cannot scale fast enough to meet demand. It's this last part that is critical. The programs cannot scale up. They can't *multiply*. This is where 10x thinking comes in.

XPRIZE embodies the exponential concept of rapid experimentation as one of the key factors in success.

Intriguingly, given the competitive nature of the prize, it is not just one team experimenting, but a diverse body of teams all approaching the problem from a different angle. This maximises the potential for coming up with an appropriate and successful solution. At the Global Learning Impact Summit, which featured all five finalist teams together for the first and only time during the competition, the diversity and breadth of the teams was on display. Let's dive into two of the finalists: CCI and RoboTutor.

Curriculum Concepts International (CCI) is a company of writers, editors, instructional designers, and technologists who have been developing educational and training programs for over 20 years. While their unique differentiator is their development system. As Josh Powe, Solution Strategist, said: "Our key innovation is the ecosystem and process for developing products at scale, not the end product." Pubbly, the internal nickname for the program, enables non-coders to develop engaging learning content in any language or subject area (similar to AnkiDroid's 'card system' which allows non-coders to create content that is then freely downloadable by users of the app). By creating an interactive system that can easily facilitate content production from multiple sources, CCI can infinitely scale the program and rapidly localize it use in multiple countries and languages.

At the other end of the spectrum is RoboTutor, which was developed by a team at artificial intelligence powerhouse Carnegie Mellon University. RoboTutor builds on decades of research and is powered by advanced technologies such as speech and handwriting recognition, facial analysis, and machine learning. Their program collects data from its interactions with children, which is then used to adapt the program to individual students and to enable data mining tools to continuously evaluate and refine the design and functionality. Amy Ofan, assistant professor of human-computer interaction at CMU said: "Our focus is at the intersection of AI and psychology…" Again, we observe the intersection of exponential technologies (facial analysis, machine learning and AI, sensors for speech recognition) along with human-focused understanding (psychology and education) that lead to breakthroughs. The winner of the XPRIZE will receive a $10 million dollar cash prize.

Ethics and success are aligned once we turn our mind to 10x thinking and solving grand challenges.

~

2.7 Leaping Into The Unknown

H. P. Lovecraft, a writer in the 19th — 20th century most famous for the creation of the existential horrors of Cthulhu and a dark cosmic pantheon, once said: 'The oldest and strongest emotion of mankind is fear, and the oldest and strongest kind of fear is fear of the unknown.' Whilst I may not be a fan of horror or subscribe to Lovecraft's rather dark outlook, I think there is something to be learned from him. Fundamentally, we fear what we do not understand. It is perhaps one of the primary foundations of racism, prejudice, and persecution. Lovecraft himself battled with his own fascination and fear of that which he considered 'foreign'. This primal 'emotion', as he describes it, has held humanity back for centuries.

How many scientists, healers and doctors were condemned as heretics or witches and burned, stymying progress for years? We have a tendency, with our 'immune system response' to attack anything that we do not immediately recognise. I do not blame anyone for this. It is programmed into us. What Lovecraft's quote reveals is just how deeply it runs. However, this is not to say we cannot overcome it. If we are to survive, to adapt, to transform, we must take a bold leap into the unknown. An incredible future awaits, that is if we choose to create it! Just because it may not be one we understand does not mean we should reject it out of hand. In fact, the odds of us fully understanding it before it arrives are very slim. As we approach the technological singularity, the moment in time when artificial superintelligence will abruptly trigger a runaway of technological growth, catalysting unfathomable changes to human civilization, changes we cannot see beyond, it will in some ways be out of our hands. I say we choose to embrace this, and all the multitudinous things that will come out of it, but let's do our utmost to point the direction of travel towards abundance.

Maxton said: 'What I've seen mostly as the main challenge to innovative thinking across the world is *critical thinking*, regardless of culture, regardless of belief. People are afraid to question because of that restriction that is already in place.' In the West, we pride ourselves in democracy and empowering people to 'think for themselves', yet we forget that many of the institutions and processes we have in place, such as a uniform state education, impede this very thing. In other areas of the world, this is altogether a foreign concept. A friend of mine, who was born in China and now lives in Thailand, said 'Many of the Chinese people are not ready for democracy. It's a nice idea, but the reality is they cannot make those decisions yet, not after years of communism and imperialism before that.' We have to remember that the unknown for one person is the known for another and vice-a-versa. However, the beauty is that critical thinking is a skill that can be learned, just as mindset, and adaptability, are muscles that can be worked.

So, what is your great unknown? Over the next coming chapters I will be arming you with techniques to overcome creative blocks, a way to define your purpose, showing you what is at stake, and defining a manifesto for humanity's future. Consider, in all of this, what leap into the unknown will you be making? Where will you boldly go where no-one has gone before?

~

2.8 Leaps® Accelerated Innovation

Every profession in the world has a toolkit. Some are literal. Look at the plumber, the engineer, the carpenter. A good professional in these fields knows what to look for when it comes to problems they have faced before and they know which tool to fetch out of their toolbox to solve it. They don't try to use a hammer to cut wood, or a saw to drive a nail. And they don't get upset if the pliers stay in the bag for a week if there was no call for their use. But consider how useful some of these tools may be in an era of digital manufacture, when 3D printing can be achieved with any material, at a molecular scale. Will we still need the same tools, or might we need to embrace, learn and try new ways of doing things? Re-skilling our workforces with a new tool kit for the world we now inhabit.

Technology is the river in which we will all be swimming: knowing the boats, paddles, and life vests for this new environment will mean the difference between drowning and thriving on the rapids. With the boats as collaboration, the paddles as rapid experimentation, and a life vest your new mindset, it is a whole new world in which we now find ourselves.

Whether you are a plumber, marketer, CEO, writer or musician, you need to have tools at your disposal, know how and when to use them to work at your best. Mark Knopfler, the lead singer/songwriter and guitarist of Dire Straits, started playing a broken left-handed acoustic guitar in his garage, a humble origin if ever there was one. But he didn't keep playing the same broken guitar. He now has over 300 (he was valued at £128 million in his heyday), in fact, and uses different ones to achieve different musical effects.

The key is using the right tool for the right problem. No doubt, as you have been reading this book, you will have considered numerous problems and barriers that are sapping your energy or inhibiting your ability to innovate and achieve all that you want to achieve. It's natural for you to do this. We all do. It's very human!

Sometimes, we are unable to think clearly and creatively because problems keep bubbling to the surface, distracting us from our ultimate ambitions. Other times, these problems are more physical. Here are some common issues that often block us. See if they resonate with you.

1. You are under tight deadlines to finish projects and maintain business as usual, so do not have *time* to spare to drive change or experiment with 'risky' new ideas.
2. You *don't understand how new technologies*, like

blockchain, AI and IOT could *apply* to your business

3. Your *financial resources are limited* and obtaining budget for new innovation is difficult

4. Losing market share with increased pressure from *competition*

5. Your organisation is spread across *departmental silos* and cross team collaboration is near impossible

6. You have a healthy pipeline of new ideas, but *lack the resources* to take them all forward and clarity to evaluate and effectively filter the right ones to prioritise

7. You have *too many complex legacy systems* in place to make any radical changes to your technology, processes and systems

8. Your *current product/service range is still successful and bringing in revenue*, so you are encouraged to prioritise resources on growing your core

9. Aware that the *energy levels* and spirit of the organisation is dwindling; 'running out of steam'

10. Launching new propositions, products or upgrades *takes too long* and you are looking for a new way to energise your team, unlock the expertise and knowledge they have and get to market faster

11. You are *looking for new ways to get closer to your customer*, embrace user-centered design

12. You are *looking for simple templates and tools* with a lean and proven framework which can easily scale across the organisation

13. Leadership and senior management are *not adapting*

fast enough to technological changes.

If any of the above feel like they hit home, then now is the time to implement some of the Leaps methodologies. Using our processes can help you sidestep some of these issues by redefining how you solve business critical challenges and explode your moonshot innovation.

Remember the acronym?

Landscape, Envisage, Agree, Prototype, Screen.

This is the five step process towards rapid and effective experimentation. In fact we have taken teams from global organisations through these steps in just 3 days, but I recommend 4 or 5 to give yourself room to breathe.

Landscape

Define your challenges and ambitions, establish your context, interview experts and share current research. Utilise this knowledge to create customer journeys and identify key areas of value/impact.

This breaks down into these five key areas:

a. Establishing the big ambition
b. Key questions ('How might we?')
c. Moments of impact
d. Mastermind insights
e. Areas identified as maximum potential

Envisage

Use proven, rapid processes and creative techniques to generate diverse collaborative solutions. Re-discover the creativity from within in a judgement-free environment of side-by-side idea exploration.

Agree

Move away from endless debates. Confidently identify the solution with the most potential via decisive decision-making methodologies. Here we used these methodologies to cut through endless debate cycles.

Prototype

Turn ideas and propositions into fully-testable, customer-facing assets using a unique combination of MVP (minimum viable products/propositions) and lean techniques.

Screen

Leverage invaluable feedback, fast. Experience first hand a series of real-time customer interactions and live-streamed interviews, to collate instantly-actionable insights.

In order to get a sense of the impact these tools and processes can have on your organisation, I want to share with you a story about a program we ran for Thomson Reuters.

The year is 2016. Thomson Reuters face the complex hurdle of creating and validating global marketing messages and developing a go-to-market strategy for a game-changing new product developed in partnership with a leader in Artificial Intelligence, IBM Watson. This program was a predictive software platform leveraging machine learning centred around data privacy and risk. It might seem hard to imagine after you have read so much about our rapidly advancing world, but even just a few years ago, there was some nervousness about whether AI would turn their audience off. Would publicly affiliating themselves with AI resonate with their key audience, would it scare, would it detract from their brand positioning? They came in with all these important questions and problems at the forefront of their mind.

This process brought together two of their biggest departments, Finance & Risk and Legal, in an intense three day workshop. For the most part these stakeholders had never met in person before despite having worked for the company, and together, for many years. This led to a very positive by-product: bringing everyone together united by the project and new approach, with a mission to explore new ways of doing things, to think bolder and to experiment with the cross-pollination of ideas from different sectors and countries.

Normally, the process of product positioning and messaging is long and arduous. Inevitably, it is handed over to a third party agency or marketing/proposition teams who then squirrel it away for months and have countless progress updates and unproductive meetings (after much chasing). Eventually, they present ideas and concepts which are either approved or rejected. Often start-overs or large overhauls are necessary to align the work with the organisation's original intention, and to top it all off there is rarely involvement with the customer in generating these approaches and concepts. Back and forth this process goes, hemorrhaging money and time. Wasted efforts, emotional disconnection, and frustration all-round, a far cry from the power of collaboration in leveraging unique abilities, the extensive pockets of knowledge sitting in the siloed islands of your teams brains.

Using the Leaps process circumnavigates these delays and disjointed meetings, where each one begins with a recap of the last, and much needed reminders of the project details due to so many distractions, other events, projects and stimulus that have taken place in between. We expect our teams and managers to run multiple and concurrent complex projects, blissfully unaware just how inefficient this can be in real terms. When compared with 100% complete and intense focus on just one challenge over a few uninterrupted days. We gathered the key stakeholders from around the world into one location. This very fact alone meant people arrived determined, ready to make a difference and to lean in to collaboration. Rather than just another day at the office, a habitual process, they were outside of their comfort zone, committed and motivated by the clock. Together in these three days, we made six months of progress.

Being in a new space allowed them to be brave, stepping outside of what they had done before. It allowed them to be creative and avoid the 'that's what we would normally do' mantra, or 'corporate would not allow this' boundaries to thinking. A freeing release to play, to pose new perspectives, to release themselves and embrace the mindsets of moonshot innovation. It allowed them to get around the corporate immune system response by being away from those systems and processes and instead focused on working as a team to achieve a collective goal at pace. It got them directly involved with the customer and not through reports and the presentations of others. They considered all kinds of strategies in this time that they would never have normally have entertained: gamification, experiential learning, new emerging technologies and channels, the thought of leveraging the crowd in new ways, dreaming of creating films, documentaries and imagining content on Netflix, collaborations with obscure niches, from giving themselves the permission to explore. Without the thought of how to justify ideas to a boss or give evidence to company executives. They were utterly freed. We had torn down multiple barriers to the innovation process.

After an intense few days, we had created and agreed on a number of concepts for this new product and had rapidly created the marketing materials that went with it: brochures, presentations, 2 short videos, event concepts, game competitions inspired by TV shows like jeopardy and AI breakthroughs like AlphaGo. Ready for the final day, we live-streamed the screening and testing of these prototype materials with specific decision makers of the target customers for the team to observe in real time. Doing this in London, New York, and Minnesota, with senior representatives from Nielsen, Tesco, Universal Music and a few others others given the materials to interact with and taken through an experience to expose their insights, reactions and gather feedback. The program team watched these key clients avidly, each with a given role, to look for key body language cues, specific word uses, questions they asked, when they leaned in, when they looked confused, when they smiled, laughed, what triggered these and look for patterns to drive their next actions. For many, this was a unique, new, and enriching experience; they connected in a profound way with their audience. Though nervous at first about their ideas not landing and being 'tested', when they saw people getting excited, or learned when parts went over their heads, it became clear just how powerful this was. Most of the senior people on the workshop only got to see this kind of feedback in dry reports which to be honest rarely invoked real change. That human interaction, made possible and instantaneous through technology, takes this process to a new level. It helped these senior decision makers to connect with what they were doing and see the human impact.

This magic of a screening day provides early indicators that are immediately actionable. It allowed them to determine where to invest, where to change strategies, and where they needed more research. The five interviews were condensed into insights they could act on right away. Using this process so early in a project meant that they could avoid 'sunken concept cost' and ensured past idea biases were avoided. Our goal to use the speed and environment as a safety cocoon for breakthrough ideas, to spark new innovations and provide a repeatable methodology and framework for the organisation to transform the way they approach problem solving. From this initial high intensity activity the team were able to identify ideas to develop and roll-out globally, the momentum, energy, buy-in and alignment provided a foundation for continued project success.

I love to inspire teams to be more ambitious, and to get closer with audiences without it costing huge investments in time and money. Many of the people who experience our programs are using the techniques, methodologies, and templates on a daily basis. Running Leaps programs across other business units and benefiting from our open source approach and online training portal to equip new facilitators inside their companies to run their own workshops.

It should be noted that working in this way asks a high level of adaptability. Those going through the workshop have to rapidly pivot from one idea to the next, respond to live feedback, and entirely let go of 'preciousness' about their ideas or knowledge (unlearning again a vital step). So, although the Leaps program was created before Adaptai and my research into AQ, there are clear parallels in how the methodologies correspond to the AQ dimensions.

I want to share another program we ran with UNIDO (United Nations Industrial Development Organization). UNIDO wanted to be seen as a modern organization differentiated from other UN agencies, with an inspired brand purpose through accelerated innovation and unifying their core messaging. Leading to a potential transformation of their business models, with a greater ability to positively impact more nations and lives. Improving the overall perception of UNIDO as a trusted enabler of the 2030 agenda. Their ideal outcome was to attract back member states to support UNIDO and see the organization's relevance as well as the need for partnerships.

The program for them was a unique opportunity:
- To increase awareness, clarity and understanding
- To bring them together through their transformation
- To align and re-engage emotionally
- To excite and strengthen relationships
- To build deeper partnerships and confidence
- To strengthen their global impact (transforming society within one generation)
- To leave a positive legacy with increased political support
- To further contribute and achieve the 2030 agenda for sustainable development, SDGs (and beyond)

Jason Slater, Head of Communications at the time and now, Head of Financial Management at UNIDO, said: "I want to find the human side of UNIDO." We worked across the breadth of the organisation, from their Director General, three quarters of the executive board, and a further 25 people from around the world. We then took a core team of ten through our original Leaps program over two and half days. Over the course of the program, we tackled a number of areas, defined messaging, including an updated brand book and templates, validated by the relevant audiences, and a stronger future-proofed brand leading to greater recognition of their impact on the SDGs. There was a tremendous engagement and spirit of collaboration in the room. "I think the commitment and the enthusiasm I've seen to this project has been overwhelming," Jason Slater said.

What were the outcomes of this accelerated process and brave commitments to a moonshot? We enabled UNIDO to communicate with one "human" voice. We united dispirit aspects of UNIDO and inspired them with the right mindsets for innovation, as well as imparting numerous tools and techniques that can be applied to future innovation efforts. I remember distinctly the moment early on in the process, when we were outlining 10X thinking and shared the moonshots video, when the Director General expressed that: failure was not acting fast enough or brave enough, we need to be more like one of the crazy ones! As I later discovered the level of animation was somewhat out of character. I think we really resonated with the challenge ahead, to transform the organisation to a new place of relevance in an ever mounting need for change across the UN. The confidence gained from this process has led to a more experimental and moonshot thinking mindset, with new projects to reimagine funding modalities through leveraging blockchain technology. I was delighted to read the call for Expression of Interest inspired by the stimulus from the program. It calls for the identification of an impact investment broker services for Sustainable Development Goals Accelerator Fund - A Circular Economy Initiative, which is being championed by two members of the original

Leaps delegates.

The proposed SDG Accelerator Fund is directed at filling the financing gap in the achievement of SDGs that are associated with the circular economy. Two exciting points of note are the thinking behind impact measurement & verification, where SMEs' financial opportunity depends on their potential financial viability and committed SDG impact. This prerequisite defines the parameters of financial flows, consequently highlighting the essential role of impact verification for its success. Impact verification is often costly, time consuming, and heavily dependent on expertise. In order to improve the efficiency of the verification process, they sight digitized impact monitoring tools will be explored. For example, blockchain technology could allow UNIDO to tokenize committed impact of SMEs in order to deliver a transparent, cost-effective, traceable, and reliable stream of information. And the second, the collaboration approach to leverage private finance, through the partnerships forged with the investment community, institutional and impact investors are leveraged to secure private finance for suitable SME projects. This leveraged finance will feed into the creation of the SDG Accelerator Fund, featuring an initial target investment of US $5-50 million.

What delights me is not necessarily the specifics, (though they are really quite cool) but the very fact the organisation is experimenting with new ways of doing things, piloting and developing the freedom and talent within to learn by doing.

Disclaimer: The comments and views expressed herein are those of Jason Slater and do not necessarily reflect those of UNIDO.

So, now you have read a couple of real life stories of impact. Here's a small flavour of how it's done.

In our five step process, we utilise seven key methodologies, all available with online training resources to learn and access the many templates to accelerate your moonshot innovation. These are tried and tested techniques, a collection of strategic, creative and group activities, refined over a decade of designing and running workshops around the globe:

Double 4s®
Unlock the best of your mind

3-5-10®
Working alone, together

'How might we?'
Challenge mapping

Moments of impact
Identify valuable interventions

Weighted Mapping Matrix
Rapid agreement

'Master Minds'

Expert interviews

'Lightning Demos'

Creative baking

One of my favourite idea-generation methodologies is a process we call Double 4s®. This technique is grounded in divergent thinking principles, which encourage spontaneous, non-linear creation. Double 4s® is particularly useful when first tackling a specific and well defined challenge and does a great job of unlocking creativity. I'm going to walk you through this process in greater detail, as I think it is an empowering group exercise. You can do this with your team or perhaps colleagues with whom you're looking to potentially collaborate.

To use this technique, you will need blank sheets of A3 paper, a bunch of Sharpies (other pens will work, but we like big marks, for bold and simple ideas) and, of course, a group of participants with a shared challenge or opportunity.

Step 1.

Make sure that the group has established a clear challenge in the landscaping phase and this is what everyone is focused on. Outline and remind the group of this specific challenge before you begin.

This is where we will be focussing on your ideas and

initial solutions. Make everyone in the group aware that you won't critique or evaluate the ideas until everyone has generated ideas and we have had a chance to build on them. This circumnavigates the group critics, who tend to hold innovation back by offering feedback before a project has even got off the ground. There's nothing wrong with feedback, of course. Nor with realism. But, it needs to come at the right stage in the creative process.

Step 2.

Introduce the next phase – we are now going to create some potential ideas and solutions.

Give the participants up to 5 minutes to make notes on blank paper in response to the collective grand challenge. They can write down comments on, for example, what matters to them, what they have gained so far during the landscaping. Remind them to think back to the key questions and utilise any of their background knowledge. What's working and how we might do things differently.

Read the room – if 5 minutes is too long you can end the session a little earlier. I often find 2-3 minutes is ample.

Step 3.

To remove any personal sense of pressure to create a winning or complete solution, ask the group to watch a short video. It should be a video that has some tangential relationship with the task at hand. For example, it could be an inspirational piece about moonshot innovation or working in teams (I highly recommend *'where good ideas come from'* by Steven Johnson, which can easily be found on YouTube).

This acts as a first stage distraction. This is one of the main components in this process. In creating a purposeful distraction in the middle of the ideation process, it allows participants' brains an opportunity to subconsciously work on the given challenge.

When you were in school, did your teacher ever say to you that you should read the entire exam paper before answering any of the questions? This is really sound advice. The brain, once it perceives a question, cannot stop itself from working on it. In fact your brain literally has to answer any question it is asked. This is why negative questions such as 'Why am I such a failure? Why can't I do this?' are so damaging. The brain will sieve through all your memories and find reasons to explain your apparent defects. However, when we use this positively, to allow us to ponder solutions without even having to consciously grasp at them, it becomes empowering. As you are writing an answer to one exam question, your brain is already subconscious working through the next. Now you know the secret!

This technique allows us to bypass the rational part of our brain that inhibits true creativity. Albert Einstein once said: 'Why is it that I get all my best ideas while shaving?'

The answer is that while his attention was on something else, the other creative part of his brain was relaxed, and could connect the dots that he might have struggled to do consciously. Many creatives talk about how they get their best ideas just before bed or in the shower; it's a similar thing.

Make sure you let everyone in your team know they have the permission to be creative. There's no point, after all, assembling an innovation team and then throwing up barriers or discouraging them. We were all born with a great gift – the ability of thought. These workshops and sessions, the here and now, is the time to embrace and experiment with those thoughts.

Step 4.

Hand out blank sheets of A3 paper, and instruct everyone in the group to fold a single sheet of paper in half twice – creating four sections.

Once they're ready, instruct all participants that they have 4 minutes to fill out 1 idea per box; this will result in up to four different ideas addressing the challenge at hand.

We are not looking for works of art, this is a time for sketching images, stick people, smiley faces, boxes, and words. These are all acceptable. Don't feel embarrassed if your doodles are not Da Vinci's. That is not the purpose of this exercise. The purpose is to quickly convey ideas. Having the four blank panels on their paper gives participants a concrete visual of what they need to fill with concepts and ideas.

The time pressure and working in silence is a key driver. Ask everyone to kindly work alone. This allows each person to think and collect their own thoughts. We're going to talk more about working alone when we come on to the next methodology I'm going to share with you, 3-5-10®.

At 3 minutes give a soft time check – '3 mins gone, 1 min left'.

Step 5.

At the end of the four minutes, ask participants set aside their paper.

Step 6.

Here we have a 10 minute intervention where we change the energy and dynamic of the room.

The facilitator, you, should ask everyone to stand and to move to a new area in the room. Pick out some volunteers and begin to ask them questions unrelated to the creative challenge. Questions such as:

- Does anyone have a pet?
- Who has watched a film in the last 2 weeks?
- Has anyone read a book in the last month, or reading one now?

As soon as there is a volunteer for the first question – ask them if they would be able to tell

the group about their pet, the film, the book for *just 60 seconds.*

The pet's name, personality, their favourite thing about them...

The film – who was in it, what was it about, what did you like? Same for the book.

It's important to ask that the other group members listen attentively.

Repeat this 2-4 times, depending on the size of the group and time you have

Why is this important?

This intentional break again disengages the conscious part of the participants' brains from trying to solve the specific challenge, allowing their subconscious mind to unlock deeper insights. At the same time, sharing personal stories increases groups inter-relationship, cohesion and trust.

Sticking to 60 seconds for the storytelling is also key, not giving too much information, just a spark. After each story ask the rest of the group, going round in a circle what they remembered about the story. After the second and third story share, the listening skills become more honed, and building upon each others' memories sets an important primer for teamwork collaboration and how different parts resonate with different people. Over the years I have found the emotional connections, the emotional parts of the stories, when shared with passion, speed, energy, and movement, help enrich the group's creative frequency.

Step 7.

Now ask participants to return to their places and turn over their original sheets, or take another sheet of paper if they prefer, and fold it once again into fours. Then instruct them to repeat the initial task with another 4 minutes to come up with four new ideas related to the original challenge at hand.

Participants often return to the challenge with renewed energy after taking a cognitive break.

The second set of four ideas is often more diverse, more creative, and the ideas arise more easily. Remind the delegates – they don't need to fill out all the boxes, and conversely if they have more than 4 ideas and are able to develop them in the time, they can grab another sheet and sketch away. At the end of this section your team will probably have generated a large number of potential ideas and solutions. We see on average over 50. That is leveraging the room's talent!

Final step: Converge and refine.

Sharing ideas after completing this individual ideation phase to further enhanced ideas. We call this 'pair share'. To unlock deeper insights and generate new adjacent ideas, ask everyone to pair up – (It is good practice to change the pairs at every opportunity throughout Leaps workshops).

Each person is given 2 to 3 minutes to share and walk through their ideas. Instruct the other person to listen actively. (This skill has been primed during the midpoint intervention for this very moment) It's important that the listener pays attention, and that the speaker is allowed to go through every idea before diving into one specific idea and 'bouncing'. At the end of the session, the sharer should ask the listener:

- What did you like about any of these ideas?
- Which one do you remember?
- Which one might have the potential to best meet the key questions and our ambition?
- Which one is really bold, truly ambitious?

Now it's time to swap over. Take a further 2 to 3 minutes to allow the other person to share. As a pair, discuss and highlight those ideas which have promise, those you would like to explore further. Be sure to identify if a new idea has emerged from the conversation (which is super, super common). Combining, adding, and merging elements from different ideas into bigger concepts and themes.

Following this, give the pairs time to work up their favorite and most promising ideas, one per A3 sheet. They are then ready for the 'Lightning Demos' and 'Museum Wall' group evaluation and enrichment phases of the whole envisioning process.

The 3-5-10® Principle

Put simply;
3 mins alone
5 mins in a pair
10 mins as a group

If you want to further amplify the power of Double 4s, or indeed any group content and information gathering, then the Leaps 3-5-10® principle, which is a beautifully simple methodology grounded in dozens of research-backed studies is a perfect companion. Developing an idea alone and then sharing it in a structured environment is often the best way to ensure quantity and quality outputs, rather than everyone trying to debate an idea in the normal brainstorming sessions. Fiction authors are a great example of this process. Yes, they take feedback from editors, publishers, beta-readers, but the initial creative process can only be done alone in isolation. Remember, feedback is good, but it must come at the right time or it interferes with our creativity.

Collaboration and group buy-in are crucial in the

contexts of where we work. Imagine if you were trying to get an internal company policy off the ground but the majority of your staff disagreed with it. Wouldn't that be an uphill battle? One that is probably not worth fighting in the long run. So, how do we get people on board, thinking in tangent? 3-5-10® is beautifully simple and especially useful in gathering group data, insights, information and ideas in a lightning fast way. To implement this technique, you will need paper or sticky notes for each participant, and bold pens or markers.

As with Double 4s, be sure to clearly define the challenge or task that will be the focus of the group. Ensure that each participant understands how their input, ideas, and insights should apply to the challenge. Again, to get people in the right mindset, ensure you have shared the mindset scorecard and as a further stimulus why not show them the moonshot thinking video if you have not done this already?

Step 1.

Ask participants to spend 3 minutes working in isolation and silence on the given challenge or problem, recording the ideas and solutions they come up with in simple note form. There's no minimum or maximum number of ideas, and participants are encouraged to freely jot ideas down however they wish, knowing they won't be asked to share them with the whole group in raw form.

People often jump to trying to share information and ideas before they've worked out their thoughts. This is ineffective at best, wastes time and can often be counterproductive.

Partly because the ideas have not been allowed to gestate yet, and partly because there will always be people ready to shoot ideas down early. It's in our nature to be critical. By enforcing three minutes of solo focus, each participant can harness their own ideas without cognitive bias or concern for how they will be received by the group. Often, listening to others who are 'quick-starts' means they often have no opportunity for self-reflection before things get flowing. Understanding the pattern of divergent and convergent thinking, similar to the 'double diamond' principle of design thinking is in part the underflow of what is happening.

Step 2.

Once participants have written down their ideas, they pair up to share their ideas with a partner for 5 minutes. During this time, they are looking for commonalities between ideas, flagging those that are most interesting, doubled up data points of information and otherwise working with their partner to hone the ideas they came up with individually. New ideas often emerge in this stage and are quite welcome. The pairs anonymously record their best ideas or most critical information they want to share with the group on sticky notes, and post these on a wall for the entire group to review.

By having two people share one-on-one, we maintain a small enough group that both voices are heard.

This period allows for incomplete ideas to come together and form the next steps of a more full-fledged and enriched ideas.

Step 3.

Next, participants are given ten minutes to read the ideas that were generated by the collective, review and consolidate duplicate ideas, and group common themes together. We often offer the opportunity to ask questions, making sure they are questions with the intention of clarifying, not judgemental ones. This can produce more diversity and quality of information, insights and ideas.

We then often encourage the use of an additional technique to prioritise, consolidate and focus the vast amounts of information. We like the fast and simple technique 'Dot Vote'. (You can find out more about how we do this online).

Optional Step 4.

In this optional step, everyone is asked to identify which two or three ideas are key based on an agreed-upon set of evaluation criteria for the specific challenge. They note their top two/three ideas by marking ticks or, ideally, placing small sticky dots directly on the notes. This enables them to quickly and silently record their votes and harnesses the energy of the entire group.

To minimize the self-censoring that often occurs when it comes to sharing in front of a large group, this phase of anonymous sharing and quiet review of ideas is crucial. The anonymity also gives participants outside of traditional "speaker" roles to voice their ideas. For example, rather than hearing from those at the top of the company, or individuals thought of as "creative," this stage allows for the ideas of participants like interns and 'quieter' staff to be heard.

Diversity, in all senses, can only strengthen the creative output of an organisation.

At Leaps, we have seen how our 3-5-10® approach unlocks deeper information, surfaces unique ideas, encourages sharing, and fosters innovation. It works especially well with the Double 4s®, and can be further woven with other approaches and situations we face in group problem solving.

We have found this methodology is so robust, easy to understand and implement it can be used is so many ways. You may well have followed similar stages in the flow of your career without realising it, or being fully intentional. Naming a process and having a common language for the approach to solving problems is key, it breeds rapid understanding, clarity of contribution and expands and gathers the value from across departmental, expertise and cultural siolos.

Using these techniques can help you greater leverage the creativity, knowledge and deep insights inherent in yourself and your team whilst simultaneously bettering communication and building up those bonds of trust and sharing. Of course, if you have interest in finding out more about Leaps from this glimpse into our ways of doing things, our methodologies and how you might learn more, do have a nose on the website (www.discoverleaps.com). However, the main point of sharing is to inspire you to think about your innovation and creative processes, how you can rapidly experiment without being inhibited by common barriers, and how you can harness the exponential potential of your team and emerging technologies.

We are building a tribe of Leaps transformers, those equipped with the mindsets, tools and ambition to leverage our principles and methodologies. To help people, teams and organisations prepare for tomorrow, to embrace moonshot innovation. If you have been inspired and motivated, if you want to do more with less, if you want to build your skill set to run programs like these, we have developed online training just for you filled with videos, resources, templates and materials.

As the subtitle of Jake Knapp's book *Sprint* implies, the aim of all of this is to do it in a short space of time. I want to share another impact story, one sparked from just one 6 hour program. At the time, Paul Polman was Unilever's CEO. Under his leadership, Unilever set a target to decouple its growth from its overall environmental footprint and improve its social impact through the Unilever Sustainable Living Plan. He very publically stood at the forefront of the global goals, caring deeply about the environment and the principles behind the 2030 agenda and the SDGs. This philosophy was an important driver for the organisation.

I should say here that Unilever run lots of workshops. They have numerous facilitators, processes, and methodologies and this is a big part of their process. Our intent, through our one-day 'expanding your horizons' program, was to tie the activities directly into the UN SDGs, using specific thinking tools, and stimulus. We turned this from being about embracing technology (for technology's sake) to being about moving the needles on those goals and how exponential technologies could be a catalyst to do it at scale. We took a small team of 12 from the power brand Dove, through our guided sessions to dig deeper into their global impact, looking at how they can future proof the brand, and re-define the way their customers engage with their brand, from the experience, packaging, and levels of personalisation. How, with the freedom to think big underpinned by technology, they might be able to transform plastic waste, how they might be able to run rapid experiments and leverage the crowd in new and exciting ways to solve problems. Create content and shape campaigns and products for the future.

Dove is a brand I have admired for many years, their philosophy, connection to real people and diversity and inclusivity values. However, like many large organisations the commendable connection from board or departmental signup to frameworks like the global goals, the voluntary Global Compact Initiative for CEO commitment, and others, did not get to the outer reaches; the desperate corners of the workforce left many gaps in awareness and understanding of what this really means. How this changes their daily activities and how it influences their projects on a practical level.

The work we did with Dove and many other organisations proves you don't need months and months of time and hundreds of thousands of dollars to start your moonshot innovation journey, you simply need to make a bold leap. And doing so with the direction and intent to shift the needle on the global goals could not be better for society, the environment and for the economic future of your organisation. Remember the world's biggest problems are the world's biggest business opportunities!

How Might We?

Across the chapters of part 2 I have endeavoured to shift from building the *why*, the inspiration and awareness in part 1, to detailing more practical tips on how to implement and apply your energy and resources. As a final act, I'd like to share another technique with you now to help your innovative process.

'How Might We?' It is a simple question that works as an invitation stem in 'challenge framing' and 'challenge mapping'. Sid Parnes first introduced the invitation stem 'How Might We?' in his 1967 book entitled *Creative Behavior Guidebook.* Each of the three words play a role in spurring creative problem solving. The 'How' part infers there are solutions — it provides creative belief. 'Might' encourages an experimental mindset, with ideas that might or might not work. 'We' instills the idea that we are a team who can build on each others' ideas. This question is a proven way to catalyst solution-thinking.

We use this method throughout a number of stages during the Leaps process; especially during interviews where individual note taking enables easy grouping and removes judgement.

It takes practice and time to become a master and create valuable and rewarding HMW questions. It's all about a balance of focus. You need to create a How Might We question that is broad enough that there are a wide-range of solutions, but narrow enough that the team has some helpful boundaries. There is a proverb: 'Limitation is the mother of creativity'. Here are some examples to help guide you with this exercise:

Too narrow:
"How Might We create a cone to eat ice cream without dripping"

Too broad:
"How Might We redesign dessert"

Better:
"HMW redesign ice cream to be more portable."

Exercise:

Use the HMW methodology to ask yourself how you can incorporate this kinds of workshop methodology into your work. Can you have a meeting once per month? What key people (from across the entire spectrum of the company) would you invite to such a meeting (we recommend 8 or less people, 10 at most).

Congratulations, you have reached the end of Part 2: Exponential Leadership. You've learned about how to deal with, and in fact thrive on, the changes that are coming, how to rapidly experiment and how to build your moonshot mindset. In Part 3, we'll talk about taking responsibility for the future we want.

~

PART 3:
TAKING RESPONSIBILITY FOR THE
COLLECTIVE FUTURE WE WANT

~

3.1 Global Ambition – leaving no-one behind

To me, the purpose of technological progress is not to advance to the point where we leave all our competitors in the dirt. It is not one upmanship.

There is already a large gap emerging between those who have access to and fully embrace technology and those who like things the way they were. This is, in part, a generational gap, but it is far broader and more complex than that. It is cultural, geographical and political. I think there are many people who believe that one day the fad of social media is simply going to die down, or that AI will be made illegal once we realise we're making the next Skynet, rather than seeing AI in the future the same way as we view electricity today. Of course, it would be easy to think in 'them and us' terms, and to see these people as change-blockers, but that is not a particularly helpful approach. I want to instead coax and tantalise these people to embrace change, direct the potential of technology to the right path, fear the future a little less, and to see the value it can add to their lives. I want to help people to adapt.

Part of the second phase of exponential technology, the 'deceptive' phase, is this idea that the value of technology is not immediately apparent. Some so called 'experts' do not yet have a full grasp of how 5G, AI, robotics, sensors, and digital manufacture, and the way these things are going to interrelate. So, how can the overworked office employee, uncertain of their job security, whose main priority is getting through another week at work and paying rent, see the big picture?

Each year I attend the Abundance 360 conference, which is currently in its seventh year. Peter Diamandis shared in his introduction to the 2019 conference: 'In year twenty-five it is going to be almost impossible, unfathomable, to understand what we can do.' It is making that possibility concrete and positive that is going to be the real challenge. How can we improve people's everyday lives, not with simple convenience, and not just in the West, but worldwide and in meaningful ways? If we could use 3D printing to solve the housing crisis, for example, I'm fairly sure there would be drastically more interest and buy in.

How do we help and support all people adapt to this new world? I believe this is part of our role as exponential leaders. It's not just envisaging the world and striving to create it, but leading people towards it and showing them the benefits. Let's not pretend it's all going to go swimmingly, there will be periods of turbulence and tribulation along the way. If recent political upheavals in the West are anything to go by, it's clear that our nations are divided along many lines. We have also not yet fully harnessed our technological capability for the betterment of our fellow humans, because many are still in the mindset of waiting for governments to sort it out. We are entering a transitional period as we approach the singularity, the moment in time where exponential technological advancement becomes literally impossible to predict. But it is not just a technological singularity, but a psychological one, where people wake up to their true potential and autonomy, their ability to change the world of their own volition. But, we must do this, not in a monomaniacal way at the cost of everyone else, but in a way that nurtures and supports others.

Exercise:

Write down a list of ways in which your MTP could potentially 'leave someone behind'. Then, write down three ways in which you could mitigate this problem. Can you offer training, mentoring, insight? How might you encourage people to get on board with your ideas?

Picture, if you will, a harbour. There are many boats in this harbour, some large and some small. These boats are crewed by diligent, hardworking sailors. The harbour's water-level is looking a little low. The tide is out. There were times when these boats were all competing for the ever depleting numbers of fish in the water but that time is now passing, because the world is abundant once again.

The time has come for a change. The tide is coming in, swelling. Mobilising, the boats begin the process of coping with the elevating water level. Each boat is working independently, but they are all rising at the same rate, buffered by the collective water levels of the new tide. They rise at an exponential level. Every boat is going to reach this higher level, this better place. This is *co-elevation*. We bring all the boats with us. Progress for one person is potential progress for all. That is, if we don't hoard knowledge, but share it; if we don't reject new ideas, but welcome them.

Imagine if some boats were tethered by fixed and strong anchors, unable to break free, to think differently, to let go of what held them, the tools that once held them safely in storms past. The very same aids of yesterday could now, without unlearning, without severing those shackles, be the very reason they risk drowning, swallowed by the tsunami of change and rising tides. We might ask: So how did they die, how did the company go bankrupt? Well, gradually, then suddenly.

Exponential technologies are inert, until we give them meaning and direction. Let's not create division, but leverage them to unify at pace and scale. Part of taking responsibility for the future we want is also taking responsibility for the people in it; leaving no-one behind.

~

3.2 What's At Stake?

It would be easy to talk about the stakes of failing to embrace this exponential world in dystopian fashion: climate change, failed progress, human suffering, and loss of life. But to do that would be to bash you over the head with the same old 'need' mantra. In my view what's really at stake is *who you want to be and how you want to live.*

Do you want to be someone who challenges and goes beyond? Do you want to look back and think that you did all you could to be all that you might be? Everything comes back to the internal, the emotional, the deeper parts of the human condition. It is, ultimately, what separates us from animals. We are separated, into external existences and internal existences. The animal is simply what it is. We have the power to dream, to visualise a future and strive towards that future. We have the power to imagine things which are not there and make them real. This is not about harbouring guilt over the death of a species, or even our own species, but about honestly reflecting on whether you can live with yourself knowing you had the chance to positively impact humanity, to make a difference globally, and never took it.

What's really at stake is the multiple versions of *you*.

You can expand yourself by making decisions now. Don't measure yourself by what other people are doing. Don't compare yourself to the Nobel or the XPRIZE winners. Your own assessment against yesterday is all that matters. Are you in a better place than you were a week ago, a month ago, a year ago? Do you continually see your future bigger than your past, no matter your age? Is your team in a better place, your company, your community? We cannot get away from *needing* (that awful word again) the approval of certain people, especially our parents, whom most of us will go to great lengths to seek approval from even in adulthood and even when we tell ourselves we are doing precisely the opposite. But, we can try as hard as we can to remain focused on what really matters whilst having a deep connection with gratitude.

Why do I say that *you* are the most important thing at stake and not the global issues we've discussed? Well, actually in relative terms and looking at the data, we're doing quite well. We need not go very far back in history to see just how much progress we have made. 100 years ago, 1919, the world looked very different. We saw the end of World War One, the Great War, which had caused over 37 million casualties. We also saw the end of the Spanish Flu which affected 500 million people, killing approximately 50 million. If the same percentage of the population were robbed of life today, we would be looking at 300 million people dead. The headlines would be unimaginable. We lose sight, amidst the bombardment of negative news stories and fear-mongering, of just how peaceful, healthy and happy the modern world is by comparison with what has gone before.

Where we are might not be good enough, but that's living in the gap; there's always room for improvement. So, what's really at stake is the person you might have been or want to be. The story you tell yourself in a month's time, a year's time; the story you tell to your children.

In December, 2018, Virgin Galactic conducted its fourth powered test flight and first space flight of its commercial SpaceShipTwo, VSS Unity. Not only was this the first human spaceflight to be launched from American soil since the final Space Shuttle mission in 2011, but it was the very first time that a crewed vehicle built for commercial 'passenger' flights reached space. On the completion of this test, Sir Richard Branson released an open letter to his grandchildren via a *video*, where he passed on some advice given to him by his father: "By keeping a childlike sense of adventure, [life] will, indeed, be wonderful."

It is the power of a child's imagination, their curiosity and wonder, that naturally embodies the mindsets of exponential leadership, and indeed adaptability. By seeing experiments and challenges as opportunities for creative play, by embracing ambiguities and polarising ideas, by shifting to a mindset of self-belief - we can become more adaptable and ready for the world of tomorrow. Healthy children, you notice, never have a problem with self-belief! And they can turn on a pin, pivoting effortlessly to new things, absorbing new information with the ease of a sponge.

If we lose this sense of wonder, we lose what it truly means to be human. Sir Richard Branson cites this advice as what has driven him throughout his entire life: "creating businesses" and "embarking on many adventures". It is a sense of profound *optimism*, that life is good and can be made even better. Life *is* an adventure and one worth having.

"Your lives will be transformed by space," he says. "And it will give your generation the planetary perspective on which the future of humanity rests. That we're all in this together. Fellow travellers in the spaceship Earth." It's an oft repeated sentiment, especially by those who have experienced space first hand, yet never has it been more relevant than now, when we seem so eager to draw arbitrary dividing lines and walls between us.

"Virgin Galactic has shown that when you set off on important and challenging adventures, exceptional people come forward to join you on your journey. People who are consistently by your side and on your side. People who share your dreams and who help make them reality."

Which legacy do you want to leave? One of adventure, change, and bravery, or one of hesitation and fear? Which story do you want to tell your grandchildren, or your students, or your nephews and nieces?

You are what's a stake.

And the stakes have never been higher.

Exercise:

Write a letter to your potential grandchildren (or actual grandchildren), or else someone you want to pass something on to, about your journey so far. At the end of the letter, fill in the blanks with two major things you would have liked to have achieved and be able to tell them about.

~

3.3 Act Now – Defining Your First Leap

In the modern world, we tend to encourage reactive thinking. Social media is also a catalyst for this. We experience mass outrage because a certain image or video has been circulated on Facebook or Twitter, and this is often used to galvanise people into action - donating to charities or signing petitions.

I am not condemning this. It is a very human thing. It is good to be outraged by atrocities. I quoted Dan Sullivan earlier: 'Your eyes only see, and your ears only hear, what your brain is searching for.' Once something enters our consciousness, it becomes this kind of obsessive pattern that our brain keeps returning to find. However, to make the change you want to see in the world sustainable and lasting, and to make a real impact, your decision to act has to be rooted deeper than a simple reflexive response to stimulus. Acting for the betterment of humanity is, strangely enough, may not be about an external situation at all. It isn't about the distressing image of the baby on the beach or of the lion being shot, it's *within*. It is a conscious, fully-aware decision that you make. It is something that you *want* to do, not that you feel obligated to do because everyone else is doing it, or because social pressures dictate that it seems like the right thing. This is why there is no point throwing yourself at Grand Challenges you care nothing about. You have to define your Massively Transformative Purpose first to see what the true reason for your or your company's existence really is, and then direct your energies accordingly.

You don't need to wait for a trigger. Be open to it happening, to discovering it, to that change occurring within you in an organic way. Don't beat yourself up about whether you are doing anything to save the planet because all your friends have signed up for animal rights campaigns following a catastrophic event. We need to move away from this guilt-trip approach towards something more wholesome and real.

Christopher Nolan, the acclaimed British film director, once said in his film *Inception*: 'I believe positive emotion trumps negative every time' and I think he is right. It is far more energising and powerful to be inspired, to be driven, to be focused, than to be outraged. Of course, anger and a sense of injustice can be a good spark to set your fire going, but they are not great resources for long term commitment and sustained innovation. Negative emotions tend to block us creatively, narrowing our thought processes to fight or flight duality. Have you ever heard the phrase 'He was so angry he couldn't see straight'? This is almost literally true. Our brain is a selective organism that will shut down parts that it deems unnecessary in certain situations. Don't fall prey to this. Become expansive and let the positive energy of change flow, alter your frequency and drive your actions.

I would encourage all of you to act on what inspires you, not simply to react to what's in the news. You may have begun to define your MTP (or you may already have one), let this guide you when it comes to deciding what kind of moonshot you want to undertake. At the same time, start to internally behave in accordance with the principles of exponential leadership, adapting how you think. The action starts internally first, then becomes manifested externally. If we think back to Maxton's story, he did not immediately leap to the end result of influencing vast numbers of young people, but slowly, over time, through acting on his principles and thirsting for more knowledge, built up his understanding and worked his way to the position where he could make that difference. The mindset comes first and if nothing else from this book, should be the key takeaway principle.

This process will take you on a path of imagination, from curiosity about things, to reevaluating who you spend your time with, what projects you get involved in and create. Make the first move, don't wait for something terrible to happen for you to start caring. Tumble down that rabbit hole with Alice and discover new horizons.

The best time to act is yesterday, the second best time is now.

It's time to define your first leap.

Exercise:

What interests you? What do you want to find out more about? Write down some of these things and explore how some of them may be connected. What could you do RIGHT NOW to find out more about them? Start with curiosity.

~

3.4 Manifesto For Innovation-Led Sustainable Change

This section is about taking responsibility for the collective future that we want. How often are we told that we shouldn't 'want' something as children. 'I want doesn't get' is the commonly repeated idiom. Wrapped up in our psyche is the idea that wanting is bad, a selfish thing. However, I think wanting is an important and powerful thing. Our wants are linked to our expectations, and only with expectations can we create the future. Dan Sullivan unpacks these ideas in great depth in his book *Wanting What you Want* (2015). We want to be wanted, by other people, in both a business and personal sense. We *don't* want to be needed, as this is 'needy' and unhealthy. Yet, we still have this massive hangup about wanting things. It's materialistic to want things. Or worse, it's idealistic to want progress.

Dan changed his whole practice as an individual to becoming a great 'wanter'. He started to write down all the things he wanted *without* the usual justification attached. Justification devalues wants. As soon as we start saying 'I want world peace because that's the morally right thing', we actually invalidate our own emotions. Dan journaled his wants every day for 25 years, freeing himself from those negative childhood memories where wants were suppressed or discouraged. The payoff has been absolute focus and clarity, internal freedom, and massive creativity.

You see, it's okay to want to change the world because you want to, to say to yourself: 'That's the world I want to create, the world I want to live in'. There is a lot of language at the moment around need. We 'need' to change the world, otherwise we are all going to die or else regress to the Stone Age. We need to fix the inequalities in the world or we are an awful, base society, no better than animals. We need to be better. It has become this kind of self-flagellating mantra that only really achieves species-wide guilt.

The differences between needing and wanting could not be more profound. If you need something it is external - it is based on scarcity, reactive, and is fear-based. Want is internal. It is an emotion of freedom and abundance. The desire to change things should come from within, from wanting, not from fearing and needing to do it. If we think we 'need' this to happen to the planet, isn't that an unhealthy relationship?

Wanting may be able to bypass politics. In this world where everyone is 'needing' and competing for status, popularity, and resources, the flipside is wanting things to happen, using teamwork, technology, and collaboration.

This initial difference in mindset sets a very different course for an individual or organisational future.

If there's one thing I want to impress upon you, it's that the responsibility you're taking should not be taken through need and obligation but through want. You don't need approval or permission. It doesn't need to be certified.

What *is* the collective future that we want? What is the manifesto? Well, the achievement of the SDG's paints a future world, the kind of world *I want to live in*. I don't need to read any more than two words: zero hunger. I don't need to think about it too hard. I don't think anyone does except maybe a psychopath. *Of course* we want this collective future. I want it for myself, and I want it for friends and family; I want it for the entire species. The shift to 'how' is often where we get stuck, but if you have a big enough MTP, surprising people will show up in this collective future, just as Sir Richard Branson observed in his Virgin Galactic video. The MTP is a uniting vision. Believe in zero hunger and others, who share that same purpose, will rally to you. The MTP is the flare gun shot rocketing into the air, flying colourful and brilliant atop the hill, calling for aide, for those who care about what you care about.

One of the big questions of the future, and where much of the 'need' language often arises, is sustainability. Things are shifting. Previously, sustainability was (in a corporate sense) only looked into after business was done. The past attitude of many large scale organisations was: *We do business and make money (the important thing as capitalists) and then from our surplus we'll do social and environmental things.*

When I think of 'sustainability' and sustainable change, to me it is about balance. As Wiki describes it: it is the very process of maintaining change in a balanced environment, in which the exploitation of resources, the direction of investments, the orientation of technological development and institutional change are all in harmony and enhance both current and future potential to meet human needs and aspirations. For many in the field, sustainability is defined through the following interconnected domains or pillars: environment, economic and social, which according to Fritjof Capra is based on the principles of Systems Thinking.

The manifesto for this collective future is not about before and after. It's all one thing. One entity. Plenty of organisations have now left the old model behind. *Doing good is good business.* And when we say good, I mean by the environment, by people, and in terms, of course, of economic growth. Thinking sustainably is the only system that works long term, after all. It's in the name.

It's up to us as leaders to change our language from 'disrupt' to 'transform' - to convey a sense of energy and excitement about this 'rising water level' of change and development. We have to think about how we use our words, how we share things with other people. The wake and impact of exponential leaders is and will be profound. Think of the boats again, the ripples of them passing to and fro in the bay affect other boats. Just how wide-reaching are those ripples of the exponential leader? As mentioned in Part 2, one of the reasons we measure Community as part of AQ Environment is that our AQ score affects other people around us. If we become more adaptable, we actually can influence other people to become more adaptable too.

As you may have gathered, while technology is key to our future, it's not the only key factor. We are the custodians of a process riding the waves of change and we have to do it in such a way that it perpetuates an energy of renewal. If it's exhausting, if we are fighting every step, we'll fail. You see people with placards railing against the government, institutions, organisations, policies. I admire them, their tenacity and dedication. But this is ultimately more of the same retrogressive *combative* approach that humans have been using for thousands of years. They even describe themselves as campaigners and crusaders, missing the irony that both of these words have their root in violence and oppression. There are some who argue that the only worthwhile human progress has been earned through violence, but I disagree. Some of the most profound collective wisdom of humanity comes from individuals who were avowedly pacifist: Mohammed, Gandhi, Buddha, Christ. They achieved their aims through inspiration, grit, communication, and the exponential dissemination of their ideas. Of course, we humans have corrupted some of those ideas over time and appropriated them for nefarious purposes. That does not dilute the essential power and immortality of some of their insights into human nature.

I may be a utopianist, but I *want* this harmonious approach, and to see it more and more in our world. Must we tear down every government or organisation that disagrees with us, or can we overcome with collaboration and by showing people the wonders of what might just be? I want and choose to find the beauty. That's the manifesto of a world I'd like to live in. That I *want* to live in. I believe even in the darkest times we can find the best in people.

You may say I'm a dreamer, but now I know more than ever: I'm not the only one.

'We do not have to engage in grand heroic actions to participate in the process of change. Small acts, when multiplied by millions of people, can transform the world.'
- Howard Zinn

For much of this book I have been talking at grand scale. Global goals. Global challenges. Moonshots. Exponential evolution. Mind-blowing technology. Innovation on a never-before-seen scale. I recognise it can be quite overwhelming. My ambition is not to overwhelm but to inspire.

You see, you do not need to change the world all by yourself. The smallest of small actions, when multiplied, can gain big action. In fact, this is historically one of the primary ways change has happened, especially in a linear world without exponential technology. If every person in the world gave £1 a year to a specific charity, then that charity would make over seven billion pounds a year. Even if you just took £1 from people over a certain income bracket, the results would still be extraordinary. Small acts from a lot of people achieve big results.

**To the exponential leaders.
The pioneers.
The GAME CHANGERS.
Here's to the ones who
see the world differently.
They're the ones who are
brave, ambitious
and experimental.
While some might see
disruption and risk,
we see hope.**

The world has changed, and now more power lies at the fingertips of everyone than ever before. I want to release you from the idea of thinking that if no one else comes on board with your vision, you will not be able to make a change. Even if you feel alone, and think you are the only person acting on the SDGs, with exponential technology at your side, you can still have global impact. But know from me, you are far, far from alone. Now imagine what could be achieved with everyone acting and using exponential tech: it's an exhilarating thought.

In 1969 the American government employed 400,000 people to work on getting us to the moon, including mathematicians, computer professionals (did you know the word computer used to be the name of a profession, long before its common association to a physical box. A "computer" used to be a person who did calculations. In 1731, the Edinburgh Weekly Journal advised young married women to know their husbands' income "and be so good a Computer as to keep within it." It was very common for companies and government departments to advertise jobs as "computers" - right up to the time when the word was used for early electronic devices, and in some cases until the 1970s), astrophysicists, engineers, researchers and military personnel. It was a national act of heroic brute force and resulted in one gruelling but successful mission. This was the original moonshot. It took nearly half a million people working collectively and almost a decade to make it happen.

Now, there are lots of ways to complete our modern moonshots. Think of it as a legion of miniature rockets, each with their own unique strategy and target. These rockets have been assembled in all kinds of ways to all kinds of different specifications. We don't need a government to fund it. We don't need a million people to make it happen. We just need imagination, ambition, and the right technology. Somewhere, there's a thirteen year old Indian girl who is about to set their rocket off.

Under the watchful eyes of The Futurist, she's shooting for the moon.

~

About the Author

Ross Thornley is an exponential leader, futurist, and adaptability pioneer. Living in the UK with his wife Karen, their two dogs, bee hive and rescue chickens, he balances the rapid technological world with a peaceful life in the New Forest, where they grow dozens of fruit and vegetables for their simple vegan lifestyle.

An eternal optimist, champion of abundance, and international speaker, he is the founder of 6 companies, including *RT Brand Communications* (2000, exit 2017), a globally trusted strategic branding agency that has worked with UN Volunteers, Thomson Reuters, Sony and numerous other blue chip clients; *Mug For Life®* (2009) a UK designed and manufactured reusable coffee cup, helping companies like HSBC, Amex, NHS, Science Museum and dozens of universities to achieve more sustainable waste policies by reduce single use disposable coffee cups and planting trees through their UK program; *Leaps® Innovation* (2017), a rapid, proven approach to moonshot innovation, idea generation and business challenges that empowers organisations to validate effective strategies, campaigns, new proposition development and solutions within days. *Adaptai* (2018) transforming the way people and organisations adapt to change. Launching the first AQ (Adaptability Quotient) assessment and personalised digital coaching platform leveraging AI.

He is a Strategic Coach FreeZone Frontiers and 10X Member, Abundance A360 Member,

and Singularity University Executive Program Graduate. Always excited by ambition, collaboration, and new models of thinking. Looking to connect ambitious people and solutions with communities, through creativity, intelligence and innovation.

His MTP is
to unite, inspire and accelerate the best of all humanity.

www.moonshotinnovation.co.uk
www.discoverleaps.com
www.adaptai.co

Printed in Poland
by Amazon Fulfillment
Poland Sp. z o.o., Wrocław

50416660R00143